The Daily Telegraph

Cornwall

in a week

GILL CHARLTON

Headway · Hodder & Stoughton

Acknowledgements

The author and publishers are grateful to John Murray (Publishers) Ltd, London, for permission to reproduce six lines from the poem *Delectable Duchy* from John Betjeman's *Collected Poems*. They would also like to thank the following for permission to reproduce photographs in this volume:

J Allan Cash Ltd: Front cover; The National Trust: pp 33, 92; The National Trust, A Besley: pp. 5, 100; The National Trust, Tymn Lintell: p. 57; Janine Hall: p. 14; Andrew Lawson: p. 30; Marion Nickig: p. 79; Dairyland Farm World: p. 109; Flambards Theme Park: p. 68; Murray King: p. 88; BT Pictures: p. 70; Cornish Seal Sanctuary, Gweek: p. 77; Sword in the Stone Ltd: p. 136

All other photographs taken by the author

Front cover: Mevagissey Harbour
Back cover: Helford River from Frenchman's Creek

British Library Cataloguing in Publication Data
Charlton, Gill
"Daily Telegraph" Cornwall in a Week
("Daily Telegraph" Travel in a Week Series)
I. Title II. Series
914.23704

ISBN 0 340 58315 0

First published 1993

Impression number	10	9	8	7	6	5	4	3	2	
Year		1998	1997	1996	1995	1994	1993			

Printed in Italy for the educational publishing division of Hodder & Stoughton Ltd, Mill Road, Dunton Green, Sevenoaks, Kent TN 13 2YA by New Interlitho, Milan.

CORNWALL IN A WEEK

Introduction

This guide is designed for visitors touring Cornwall by car who wish to see the best the county has to offer in the limited time at their disposal. We have divided Cornwall into seven areas, each of which can easily be covered in a day's drive. Within each of these 'Days' the most interesting sights, from seaside resorts and fishing villages to stately homes and theme parks, have been listed as a menu of options, arranged in alphabetical order for easy reference. From the Day's menu you can choose the attractions which hold most appeal, depending on the weather, your interests, and whether you are travelling with children. Symbols placed alongside the text will aid you in your choice.

There are over 250 attractions open to the public in Cornwall and the aim of this guide is to give a critical appraisal of the most popular attractions and help you discover some of the county's hidden gems. Our assessments of the different sights and attractions will give you a clear idea of what you can expect to see, the best time of day and year to pay a visit and, where admission is charged, whether the attractions offer value for money. As well as covering the main resorts, towns and tourist attractions, we have highlighted small gems in each area, from safe sandy beaches and boat trips to superior craft shops and places for lunch.

A circular walk of the day in each area is described in detail. Most are just over one hour long and provide an opportunity to get out of the car and stretch your legs. We have also included descriptions of particularly interesting drives which are scenic in both rain and sunshine. At the end of each Day we have given suggestions for places to stay, from country house hotels to farmhouses, and places to eat, from the best seafood restaurants to pubs with good home-made fare.

CONTENTS

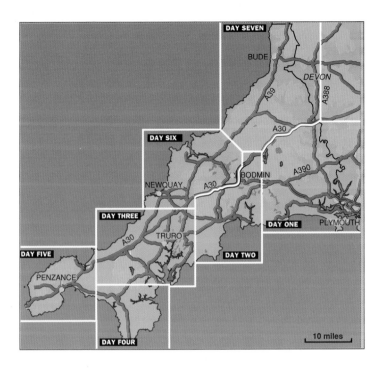

KEY TO SYMBOLS

✪	Star Attraction
☆	Well worth a visit
☆	Of interest
👣	Walk of the day
-----	Route of walk
🚗	Drive of the day
═══	Route of drive
☀	Fine weather attraction
🌧	Wet weather attraction
🏃	Enjoyable for children
ⓘ	Tourist Information Centre
◉	Lunch/snack stop
🏨	Hotel
Ĝ	Guesthouse
✗	Restaurant
🍴	Pub with good food
🍴	Pub with accommodation

👦5 Children allowed (number = from which age)

🐕 Dogs allowed

💳 Credit cards accepted

✗ Credit cards not accepted

£ Bed and breakfast under £17 per person; three-course meal under £10 a head

££ Bed and breakfast £18-£35 per person; three-course meal £11-£16 a head

£££ Bed and breakfast £36-£49 per person; three-course meal £17-£24 a head

££££ Bed and breakfast over £50 per person; three-course meal over £25 a head

1

SOUTH-EAST CORNWALL

South-east Cornwall is different in character from the rest of the county. It remains well wooded and deeply rural with ancient farmsteads dating back to Domesday times, mediaeval clapper bridges, and a web of narrow lanes connecting sleepy hamlets and winding through leafy river valleys like the Lynher. There are several historic landed estates - Antony House, Cotehele and Mount Edgecumbe - whose houses and grounds are open to the public.

In complete contrast, Polperro, perhaps the prettiest of all the Cornish fishing villages, becomes over-run with visitors in summer. But early or late in the day it is not to be missed; nor is the magnificent walk along the coast to Looe, a pleasant resort and fishing port and a good place for boat excursions and fishing trips. On a rainy summer's day you can spend an enjoyable couple of hours listening to Paul Corin's splendid collection of music machines.

If you are travelling with children under 12, Dobwalls Family Adventure Park offers the appealing combination of imaginative adventure playground, rides on miniature steam trains and an unusual gallery of wildlife paintings. Families will also enjoy the Monkey Sanctuary near Looe where Amazon woolly monkeys have been successfully bred and reintroduced to the wild.

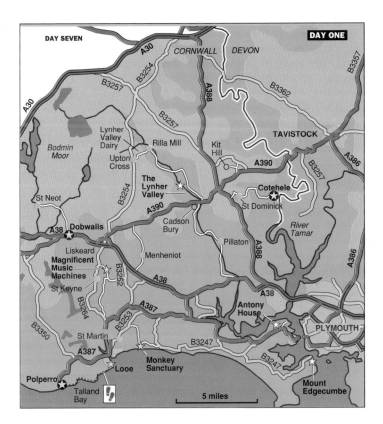

☆ ANTONY HOUSE

Lovers of fine furnishings and portraiture will particularly enjoy visiting this silver-grey stone Queen Anne mansion which stands in beautiful landscaped grounds leading down to the River Lynher. The estate has been the home of one of Cornwall's leading families, the Carews, since mediaeval times and, although it is now owned by the National Trust, it remains the home of Richard Carew-Pole and his family .

The house was built in 1711 by Sir William Carew for £1,260, and remains surprisingly little altered. The main rooms, panelled in Dutch oak, retain many of their original furnishings, giving it a very satisfying period feel. The 40-minute conducted tour is informative and comprehensive with visitors being allowed to view all the reception rooms and the main bedrooms. There is plenty of eye-catching furniture in the handsomely proportioned rooms, some dating from Tudor times although most is 18th century, including real Chippendale pieces and chairs covered with original Huguenot tapestry work and embroidered silks which came from a Vatican sale of papal vestments. The family portraits are particularly fine and include works by Reynolds, Romney and Sargeant.

Upstairs is a series of grand bedrooms including the Porch Room where Daphne du Maurier once stayed; the characterful portrait of Rachel Carew on the wall was the inspiration for her novel *My Cousin Rachel*. After the tour, visitors are let out by a back door into the grounds where, beyond avenues of clipped yew hedges, clumps of holm oaks frame vistas leading down to the River Lynher. Don't miss the dovecote, which is still in use.

Antony House, entrance on the A374 just outside Torpoint. Tel: 0752 812191
Opening times: Apr 1-end Oct, Tues-Thurs and Bank Hol Mons, plus Sun in June, Jul and Aug, 1.30-5pm
Admission: adult £3.40; child £1.70; NT members free

✪ COTEHELE

The Cotehele Estate climbs away from an enchanting stretch of the River Tamar. You will appreciate its soothing tranquillity after what can be a hair-raising drive down a succession of single-track lanes to this forgotten quayside. When the Tamar was a major thoroughfare in Victorian times, filled with barges carrying cargoes of farm produce and quarried stone to Plymouth, this would have been a bustling place. But now, even on a busy summer weekend, you will want to linger in this peaceful spot.

Expect to spend the best part of a day here, as there is a great deal to see on the estate - an atmospheric Tudor manor in lovely terraced gardens, a working mill, a branch of the National Maritime Museum, and a delightful riverside walk. If you are visiting Cotehele between June and September or on a weekend you should be prepared to wait to enter Cotehele House itself as only 100 people are allowed inside at once. At these busy times the National Trust issues timed tickets and it is best to pick up one of these at the reception beside the house before touring the rest of the estate. Follow signs to **Cotehele Quay** and park in the car park there (disabled visitors can also park near the house).

Cotehele Quay on the River Tamar

Among the cottages, former warehouses and lime-kilns on the quay is a small museum containing some interesting exhibits on the history of boat-building, river trade, and silver, copper and arsenic mining in the area. The last surviving Tamar sailing barge, the Shamrock, is moored alongside. The Edgecumbe Arms is now a pleasant café serving light lunches, non-alcoholic refreshments and ice-creams.

From the quayside, a 15-minute woodland walk alongside a stream brings you to **Cotehele Mill**, a splendid working water mill arranged on three levels. The wooden floors and shafts shake in an alarming manner as an array of belts drives the massive cog-wheels in true Heath Robinson fashion. Across the way outbuildings contain a fully equipped blacksmith's forge - there's even a fire going - and wheelwright's, saddler's and carpenter's shops.

To reach **Cotehele House** the scenic way take the field gate below the forge into the meadow and cross the stream, then walk up the track and take the left fork uphill. The woodland walk takes around 20 minutes and is particularly beautiful in the late spring. The fortified mediaeval manor, remodelled in the early 16th century, is an absorbing place for those with a sense of history. Over the centuries little has changed here; even the furnishings, including embroidered bed hangings, are 300 years or more old. Its mediaeval style survived intact as the Edgecumbe family soon found the manor house old-fashioned and built an altogether grander country seat, Mount Edgecumbe opposite Plymouth, just a few decades later. After the Civil War, it was used only as a summer retreat, a store for unwanted furniture, and a place to banish aged relatives. It's worth watching the 8-minute slide presentation on the history of the family and the estate before touring the house.

As you enter the studded oak door into the Great Hall with its spectacular trussed wooden roof, there is a strong feeling of stepping back in time. There is no guided tour, but National Trust curators are on hand to answer questions and leaflets describe the contents of each room in detail, so purchasing a guidebook is not necessary. Best of all, nothing is roped off, so you can inspect the exquisite embroidery and tapestry work at close quarters. In nearly all the rooms the walls are hung with 17th-century Flemish tapestries, arranged somewhat haphazardly so that following the allegories and mythical stories they depict is thwarted. But even if your interest in tapestry is slight, they give the rooms much period atmosphere and the figures and animals depicted are very finely drawn.

While the once-vibrant greens of the tapestries have faded to blue, the 17th-century upholstery fabrics which cover the chairs and adorn the intricately carved four-poster beds are almost as colourful now as when they were made. Most of the embroidery is crewelwork, preserved in superb condition, and the 18th-century white Durham bedcovers look brand new. It is this combination of near-period furnishings and the survival of the original lay-out that lends the house such an aura of antiquity, delighting both Victorian romantics and modern visitors. Worth seeking out too is the 15th-century clock in the chapel, one of the earliest domestic clocks in England, which still strikes the hours.

Adjoining the house is the licensed Barn Restaurant where good home-cooked food, including cream teas, is served until 4.30pm. The surrounding terraced gardens are worth a stroll, especially for the camellias and rhododendrons in late spring and the roses in mid-summer, and there are fine views over the whole valley from the top of the Prospect Tower. If you have time there is a delightful walk along the riverbank to Calstock from the quay-side car park.

Cotehele House, St Dominick, near Saltash. Tel: 0579 51222
Opening times: House open daily, except Fri, Apr 1-end Oct noon-5.30pm (earlier in
Oct as no electric light in the house)
Admission: adult £5; child £2.50; NT members free

You can paddle a single or double kayak along the River Tamar for a few hours - no experience necessary - with **Tamar Expeditions**. Depending on the tide, departures are from Halton Quay or Barnsdale where you leave your car and take a mini-bus to the starting point. After a brief instruction session you simply drift along with the current past Cotehele and Morwellham with a lunch break at Calstock. The trip takes around four hours and a safety boat follows the group. Departures: weekends only April and May; once or twice daily June - mid-September. Children over 8 and the physically and mentally handicapped are welcome. The trip costs around £12 a person; times vary daily so reserve in advance by telephoning Tamar Expeditions on 0579 51113.

DOBWALLS

Adventure parks are springing up like mushrooms all over Britain, and most fail to offer real value for money. Dobwalls Family Adventure Park is in a league apart; if you have children under 12, it can provide the best part of a day's entertainment for all the family. Like all the best attractions, it is the work of one dedicated man, John Southern, a former farmer who has turned his love of American railroads and his collection of wildlife paintings into the focal points of an extremely professionally run theme park.

Set on the southern flank of Bodmin Moor it has three elements: a family adventure playground, a miniature railroad, and an innovative and stimulating art gallery dedicated to the work of Britain's most celebrated wildlife artist, Archibald Thorburn. Aimed at good old-fashioned family fun (there are no horror rides) the adventure playground is arranged as an interconnecting trail of play for adults and children through larch and pine woods. There are tube slides, cableways, rope bridges and all kinds of sturdy wooden climbing equipment. Most popular is the Famous Five slide where parents and children can race each other to the bottom.

Weaving around the play areas are the tracks of the Union Pacific and Rio Grande railroads. Scale models of American steam and diesel engines pull up to 90 passengers around the mile-long routes, modelled on sections of the original railroads in the US, with tunnels, steep cuttings and waterfalls. The rides are great fun, and twice a day - at noon and 2.30pm - there is a Grand Parade of all 10 engines, each an exquisitely crafted model of a famous American 'Iron Horse', together with a 10-minute talk by one of the mechanics.

If viewing a collection of wildlife paintings sounds less than riveting, a tour of the award-winning Thorburn Museum and Gallery will change your mind. John Southern has been collecting the Edwardian paintings of Archibald Thorburn since the age of 11, and now has 200 of them, insured for £10 million, displayed in a most imaginative audio-visual way that appeals to both adults and children. It starts with a talk on Thorburn's methods by his niece Barbara Joan in an Edwardian parlour setting. Then you move through a series of sets which recreate most effectively the habitats and the calls of the birds and animals in the paintings: the roar of a stag, the menacing flap of an eagle's wings and the bubble and coo of black grouse, Thorburn's favourite subjects. In this way the paintings are brought vividly to life and you feel as if you are journeying from the Scottish highlands to woodland glades.

There are several other entertainments in the park: remote-controlled trucks and boats, a shooting gallery, videos of the real American locomotives in action, and an Edwardian Penny Arcade where over 30 machines, some a century old, can be operated by using old pennies which now cost 10p. There are several places for lunch: an American diner set between the rail tracks, a Victorian tea-room, and an outdoor barbecue. You can also bring your own picnic and eat lunch at tables in the park. The park is kept spotless and visitors who arrive with dogs are given a pooper-scooper!

Dobwalls Family Adventure Park, signposted off the A38, 3 miles west of Liskeard.
Tel: 0579 20578
Opening times: daily Apr 1-Nov 7, 10am-6pm; last admission 4.30pm
Admission: adult £6.50; child 3-16 £4.50; family car ticket £20

> Just a few miles north of Dobwalls is **St Neot**, a pretty village on the edge of Bodmin Moor. Its handsome Perpendicular church contains an impressive collection of stained glass windows dating from the early 16th century. Look out for the charming strip-cartoon simplicity of the scenes from the life of St Neot, a Saxon saint.

LOOE

The steep wooded valleys of the East and West Looe rivers converge at Looe, the second largest fishing port in Cornwall. The town picturesquely straddles a long narrow estuary, hemmed in beneath tall wooded cliffs. Along the quaysides coastal trawlers and fishing boats lie several deep, and you can watch the catch being unloaded and sold in the fish market. The town's heart is in East Looe, a tangle of narrow streets lined with slate-hung cottages bowed with age. Beyond the harbour is the town beach, its sands extremely popular with summer visitors, although small stones appear at low tide.

While Looe is a very pleasant place to enjoy an evening stroll, watch the fishing boats unload or have dinner, it can become very crowded in July and August. During this period it is advisable to park in Liskeard and take the train to Looe. The beautiful journey along the banks of the East Looe river is an attraction in itself. Looe has little in the way of specific sights. The 15th-century Guildhall is more impressive than the jumble of local artefacts it contains. Next to the fish market, Living from the Sea tells the story of Looe's fishermen alongside tanks containing some of the more extraordinary fish they have caught, including a 100lb blue shark on a recent visit.

Of far more interest is the new **South East Cornwall Discovery Centre** in West Looe car park just across the bridge. Its aim is to encourage visitors to explore some of the less obvious sights in the area, and in this it succeeds admirably. A 7-minute video runs through the attractions of this corner of Cornwall which stretches from the River Tamar to the Fowey estuary and up to Bodmin Moor. Interesting photographic displays alongside cover the area's flora and fauna, heritage, landscape and community life. The highlight is a series of 3-D stereoscopic views of local scenes which make you feel as if you are stepping into them. This is a good place to pick up free tourist literature on the area, including a guide to special events over the coming months, and the bookshop is excellent.

South East Cornwall Discovery Centre, West Looe Car Park. Tel: 0503 262777
Opening times: Easter-end Sept daily 10am-6pm, except Sat noon-4pm. Closed Jan and Feb, otherwise winter opening 10am-4pm; closed Sat
Admission free

> A plethora of **boat trips** operates from the quay in East Looe between Easter and the end of September. You can chug along the coast to Polperro and Fowey, up the West Looe river to Watergate, and across to Looe island, a nature reserve where you can spend two hours or the whole day. Looe also offers a wide choice of sea fishing trips. A day's shark fishing costs £20 a person (£100 a boat). There is also deep sea fishing for ling and conger eels, and half-day mackerel and pollack trips which cost around £6 a head. Contact Harry Barnet at the Tackle Shop on the Quay (tel: 0503 262189) for information and bookings.

☆ **THE LYNHER VALLEY**

If you wish to escape the madding crowds, especially in high summer, the beautiful wooded valley of the River Lynher is the place to head. It is a remote area of age-old stone farmsteads, tiny hamlets, and ancient coppiced woodland. There are some lovely picnic spots in riverside glades carpeted in wild flowers including primroses and bluebells in spring. Start or finish, if you want to see the milking, at the **Lynher Valley Dairy**, where you can see Cornish Yarg cheese being made by hand. A visit starts with a slide show in the café, followed by a guided tour of the dairy. Depending on the time you visit, you will see the curd

Foot ferry crossing to West Looe

being cut and the whey drained, the cheese rounds wrapped in the traditional nettles and, in the late afternoon, the milking of the Friesian-Holstein cows which always delights children. There's also a riverside nature trail, ponds and a picnic area but the admission cost is quite high and you may prefer simply to drop in and buy some tasty Yarg for a picnic lunch, or their pepper and herb and garlic soft cheeses, all made with vegetarian rennet.

The Lynher Valley Dairy, Netherton Farm, off the Upton Cross-Rilla Mill road.
Tel: 0579 62244
Opening times: Easter-end Oct, Mon-Sat 10am-4pm
Admission: adult £2; child £1

The next place of interest, reached along narrow country roads through the Lynher valley is **Cadson Bury**, an Iron Age hill fort. From Newbridge turn left off the A390 immediately after the bridge and turn into a small car park on the left. From here there's a lovely walk through woodland alongside the Lynher. Cross the lane and take the footpath signposted The Bury up to the top of this ancient mound. It rises 160ft above the surrounding countryside, narrowing to a flat summit shaped in a perfect oval, from where there are panoramic views over the countryside. A path leads down through woodlands back to the car park.

More far-reaching panoramic views can be had from the top of 1,000ft-high **Kit Hill** four miles away, off the A390 east of Callington. It is less atmospheric than Cadson Bury but has the advantage of a road up to the summit. From here you can see over a great swathe of Devon and Cornwall: as far as Bude on the north coast, the Tamar river and Plymouth Sound to the south, Dartmoor and Bodmin Moor and, far out at sea, the Eddystone Lighthouse.

Returning to the Lynher valley, carry on down the lane beside Cadsonbury car park to a T-junction. If it hasn't rained recently, turn left by an ancient farmhouse and go over a ford before meeting a lovely stretch of the Lynher which is crossed further down by an ancient clapper bridge. There are some lovely picnic spots on this stretch of the riverbank. Alternatively head for the sleepy village of Pillaton and **The Weary Friar**, an inn dating back to the 12th century, originally built to feed and house the builders of St Odolphus church next door. It has changed considerably since then, but remains a welcoming, homely place. You can tuck into good ploughman's lunches, home-made soup and chunky sandwiches from noon-2pm; in the evening there's a more formal restaurant serving classic English fare: honey roast saddle of lamb, beef Wellington, and steaks.

☆ MAGNIFICENT MUSIC MACHINES

A large hall next to the home of Paul Corin in the village of St Keyne contains this fascinating collection of music machines, from turn-of-the-century café orchestrions to a magnificent Wurlitzer theatre pipe organ. Paul Corin, who inherited the collection from his father, has a great enthusiasm for these self-playing pianos and organs and has restored many of them himself. Taking each music machine in turn, he gives a short entertaining talk on its background and invites you to observe its mechanics, before playing a piece of music programmed on paper rolls or punched cards. Among the fair and street organs, there is a wonderful Steinway-Welte piano which plays a Bridal March recorded by Grieg onto a paper roll at a studio in Germany's Black Forest.

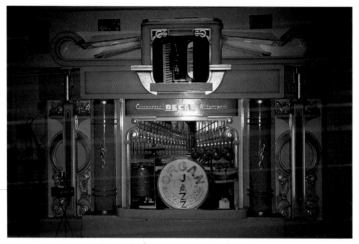

Magnificent Music Machines

The Mighty Wurlitzer theatre pipe organ, rescued from Brighton Theatre where it originally provided the soundtracks to silent films, is played by Paul himself. The range of noises it can produce is endless: church bells, a barking dog, seaside surf, and even birdsong. As the Wurlitzer is played, the black wooden slats, which occupy a whole side of the building, open up to reveal a forest of pipes of all shapes and sizes. It takes about one-and-a-half hours to hear all the music machines play, and it's a good place to cheer yourself up on a rainy day.

Paul Corin's Magnificent Music Machines, off the B3254 opposite St Keyne Station. Tel: 0579 343108
Opening times: Easter and daily May-end Oct 10.30am-5pm
Admission: adult £3; child £1.50

☆ MONKEY SANCTUARY

On a cliffside high above Looe Bay is a most extraordinary sight: a troop of Amazon woolly monkeys bouncing through the trees. For 25 years this spectacularly sited Victorian house and garden has been home to these completely captivating animals, who bear no resemblance to the aggressive temple monkeys who beg for food. Many were rescued from lives of isolation in zoos or as pets and allowed to develop their traditional tribal culture and live as naturally as possible. Breeding has been very successful and there are now 21 monkeys spanning three generations at the sanctuary.

The monkeys live in large interconnecting enclosures slung with logs, ropes and swings, with access to the trees. When the sanctuary is open they are often allowed to roam the garden and visitors are encouraged to join in their play and forage with them, but not to touch them. This is not because they might bite you but, just like humans, they do not like to be stroked and patted by strangers. Whether the monkeys are inside or out, it is fascinating to watch their group behaviour and play. They move with confidence and grace, using their powerful prehensile tails to catch hold of branches. Beneath their thick grey fur you can admire their incredibly muscular frames: Charlie, the 11-year-old leader of the colony can hang by his tail and lift a man off the ground. The keepers give a talk every hour or so, and there is usually someone beside the main enclosure to answer questions.

Inside the house, where the monkeys retreat for the odd very cold day, there is a video room where you can watch a film

Helping woolly monkeys forage for food at the Monkey Sanctuary

recording what happened to Ricky and Ivan, two young monkeys born at the sanctuary, when they were reintroduced to the wild in Brazil. It is a touching tale and it has a happy ending. To keep children entertained, the keepers run short workshops several times a day, providing arts and crafts materials to encourage children to observe and draw the monkeys. For anyone interested in wildlife, an enthralling morning or afternoon can be spent here - there is also a small British wildlife garden on the cliffs - and while the admission charge may seem a little steep, it all goes towards the high cost of running the sanctuary.

The Monkey Sanctuary, signposted on the B3253 at No Man's Land between East Looe and Hessenford. Tel: 0503 262532
Opening hours: Easter-end Sept, Sun-Thurs 10.30am-5pm
Admission: adult £3.50; child 4-14 £1.50

MOUNT EDGECUMBE

For generations this was the family seat of one of Cornwall's most important families, the Earls of Edgecumbe, who moved here from Cotehele (see earlier entry) in the 16th century. Sadly the Tudor mansion, later remodelled in neo-classical style, was hit by a bomb during the Second World War, leaving only a pink sandstone shell. The 6th Earl bravely re-constructed the interior in Georgian style and finally moved back in during the Sixties. Today the house and its landscaped park are owned jointly by Cornwall and Plymouth councils and are open to the public.

It is worth visiting the house if you have been to Cotehele and are interested in the history of the Edgecumbes, but despite the beautifully proportioned rooms which contain family antiques given in lieu of death duties, it inevitably has more the feel of a show house than an historic family seat. There is no guided tour but knowledgeable stewards are on hand to answer questions. There are a few family portraits in the magnificent hall, rebuilt on its original lines. You exit through the Earl's Garden with its lawns, terraced walks and shrubberies. Don't miss the 18th-century shell seat, covered with conch shells, mother-of-pearl, coral and quartz.

Surrounding the house is a landscaped park which spreads over a large headland directly opposite Plymouth. It contains around 180 species of trees, most getting on for 200 years, and the walks afford magnificent views of Plymouth Sound and, on a clear day, Dartmoor. Within the park there are seven acres of formal gardens designed to give an idea of the differences between English, French and Italian gardening styles. Some of the park's important collection of camellias - at their best in March and April - can also be seen here. A well written series of leaflets describes the main attractions of the park and how best to explore it and, in the old Orangery, there's a restaurant.

Mount Edgecumbe House and Country Park, Cremyll. Tel: 0752 822236
Opening times: House and Earl's Garden open Apr 1-Oct 31, Wednes-Sun and Bank
Hols 11am-5.30pm; country park open daily all year
Admission: country park free; House - adult £2.55, child £1

Whitsand Bay is a lovely place for walking, sunbathing and beach games. Turn off the B3257 beside Tregantle Fort and follow the cliffside road to a car park opposite Sharrow Point. A path opposite leads to a new metal stairway giving access to several beautiful sandy coves, revealed at low tide as the sea recedes beyond great fingers of shale. The water is an inviting brilliant blue, and this is a favourite swimming place for locals, but visitors should beware of undertow and strong currents, especially on the outgoing tide.

Whitsand Bay

Polperro

POLPERRO

 Polperro is, arguably, the most picturesque fishing village in Cornwall. It is also on nearly every visitor's itinerary, and the car park - nearly as large as the village itself - is a 15-minute walk from the harbour. Thankfully, the villagers have resisted the temptation to cash in on tourism, and there has been a deliberate attempt to conserve the look and the feel of old Polperro without turning it into a museum. The harbour is busy with working fishing boats and there's a strong sense of community, including an internationally famous **Fishermen's Choir** which usually performs on Wednesday evenings in summer on the quay or in the chapel if it's wet. Of course, there are shops full of cheap seaside souvenirs, tea rooms, and a score of pubs, but there are no flashing neon signs, amusement arcades or fish and chip shops on the quay.

The village spills down a cleft of a valley beside a stream, finishing in a jumble of whitewashed cottages which perch on rocks just feet above the water. The narrow lanes behind thread between old stone fishermen's homes, cosy centuries-old pubs, and sail lofts converted into artists' studios. Tiny flights of steep steps lead eventually to homes high above the harbour and there are enticing paths around the cliffs which shelter the inlet. In the summer months the village becomes so swamped by daytrippers that it can be difficult to appreciate its great charm. If you are planning a visit at this time try to arrive well before 10am or after 5pm when the coaches have gone.

> For lunch or an early evening drink seek out **The Three Pilchards** on the right hand side as you face the harbour. It is a cosy, friendly pub with low beamed ceilings and is popular with locals. The beer is good, as is the home-cooked food: beef and onion soup, vegetable macaroni, beef Stroganoff and fresh catch of the day. Open 11am-11pm in summer.

There is one small attraction which may amuse you - the **Smugglers Museum** in the main street. This stretch of coast was notorious during the 18th century, the golden age of smuggling in Cornwall. Inside the museum there is a former smuggler's hide entirely enclosed within the thickness of the house walls. Although the museum has been here for decades, the collection of smugglers' tools of trade is interesting and the explanations informative, if a little dusty. Also on display are some of the ingenious ways people have tried to smuggle contraband goods into Britain in recent years.

Polperro Smugglers Museum is open daily Easter-end Oct, 10am-7pm
Admission: adult £2.55; child £1

A COASTAL WALK

The cliff-top walk from Polperro to Looe is one of the most beautiful on the south coast. It takes two hours and is best done in the early evening with the sun behind you. Park in one of Looe's car parks and stroll along the quayside in East Looe to see if there's a boat trip to Polperro departing soon. If not, there is usually a taxi which will take you there for around £3.50 or a bus. From Polperro harbour turn left up a narrow lane called the Warren which climbs around the headland. Benches have thoughtfully been provided so you can admire the beautiful view back down over the village.

The path skirts the edge of the cliffs between banks covered in wild flowers. It may seem like a sheer drop from here but below are tiny cliff-side allotments where the villagers grow fruit and vegetables. The path rounds into Talland Bay, a typical Cornish hamlet of a few white-washed homes, a church and a pebble beach. In past centuries Talland was a notorious haunt of smugglers, who used the church tower to signal to ships that it was safe to unload and hid their packhorses between the church and its unusual separate tower.

Walk along the beach, from which there is safe bathing, and rejoin the coastal footpath. The tall black-and-white striped board marks the start of a measured nautical mile (there is another one behind West Looe), used by the Navy for speed trials. Ponies and rabbits graze on the clifftops and a magical stretch of coast slowly unfolds below: the late afternoon sun drawing out the colours of the rock - glorious shades of lilac, pink and grey - weathered into stacks and serrated fingers which reach out into a royal blue sea. Further along you come to a grey sand beach, reached down a steep path. Soon after this the footpath joins a quiet seafront road which takes you through West Looe and back down to the port.

WHERE TO STAY

Looe

🏠 🐴 🍽 ££ ⅄8

Commonwood Manor Hotel,
St Martins Road, East Looe PL13 1LP
Tel: 0503 262929
Open Mar 1-Oct 31
This pleasant Victorian villa stands in its own grounds high above the East Looe river. Looe harbour is a 10-minute walk away. There are 10 nicely furnished bedrooms with attached bathrooms and those at the front have magnificent views over the wooded river valley. A table d'hôte dinner is served at 8pm. Ample car parking.

Looe

G 🍽 £ ⅄

Greenoaks, *Marine Drive, Hannafore,*
West Looe PL13 2DH
Tel: 0503 262598
Open Mar 1-Oct 31
There are three rooms in this friendly guesthouse on the quiet esplanade road in West Looe, but try to book the one on the first floor which has a balcony and magnificent views over the coast as far as Rame Head. A comfortable sitting room for guests also shares the sea view. There is a free car park at the rear - a big plus in Looe - and the coastal path to Polperro is a 5-minute walk away. Excellent breakfast, including fresh kippers and haddock.

Menheniot

G 🍽 £ ⅄6

Tregondale Farm, *Menheniot, Liskeard*
PL14 3RG
Tel: 0579 342407
Closed Christmas
Stephanie Rowe has been taking in guests for 20 years in this deeply

rural part of south-east Cornwall, just a 10-minute drive from the A38. If you're alone you will even be invited to join the family in the kitchen for some good farmhouse cooking: roasts with all the trimmings, hot-pots, pudding and cheese board. The two bedrooms (one with a third bed) are prettily decorated, each with a lovely modern bathroom with bath and shower. Children can visit the pedigree South Devon calves, and daughter Amanda takes pony rides.

Pelynt

G 🍽 ££ ⅄16

Trenderway Farm, *Pelynt, near*
Polperro, Cornwall PL13 2LY
Tel: 0503 72214
Open all year
Situated in tranquil countryside at the head of the Polperro valley, this lovely 16th-century farmhouse surrounded by great granite barns offers very superior accommodation. Lynne Tuckett has decorated four bedrooms - two in a converted barn - with the flair of a professional interior designer. Bathrooms are the size of some hotel bedrooms and contain separate shower cabins as well as baths.

There's a sitting room for guests and a sunny breakfast room in a conservatory where eggs from the farm's free range chickens and sausages made by the local butcher are served at 9am.

The warm welcome and stylish decor beats country house hotels hands down.

St Keyne
⌂ ✕ ⚲ ▭ £££ ⚲

The Well House, *St Keyne, Liskeard PL14 4RN*
Tel: 0579 342001
Open all year
This Victorian country manor, built by a tea planter who wanted to capture the sunlight in his home, stands on a rise above the tranquil valley of the East Looe river. It is run in a friendly, country house style by Nick Wainford who presides behind the intimate bar in the evenings. The eight pleasant bedrooms and the public rooms are suffused with light, and all have lovely country views. The well-tended gardens contain an all-weather tennis court and a heated outdoor pool. The restaurant, open to non-residents, serves refined versions of traditional English dishes: Cornish crab bisque, fillet of lamb rolled in English mustard served with rosemary gravy, escalope of turbot poached in cider with leeks, and rhubarb crumble and custard. Good wine list. Last orders: lunch 2pm; dinner 9pm.

St Martin-by-Looe
⌂ ⚲ £ ⚲

Bucklawren Farm, *St Martin-by-Looe PL13 1NZ*
Tel: 0503 4738
Open Mar 1-Nov 30
This comfortable farm guesthouse stands high on a cliff a few miles east of Looe. There are lovely sea views from several rooms and from the garden where guests sit out on summer evenings. Bedrooms are simply furnished, most with attached bathrooms. There is also self-catering accommodation in converted stone farm buildings, and if you choose this you can still dine in the farmhouse which serves good home cooking. There are also good restaurants in East Looe, a 10-minute drive away.

Talland Bay
⌂ ✕ ⚲ ▭ £££ ⚲

Talland Bay Hotel, *Talland-by-Looe PL13 2JB*
Tel: 0503 72667
Closed Jan
This low white country house, parts of which date back to the 16th century, is superbly situated on a hillside above Talland Bay. Many of the rooms have views across the lawns to the sea, and all are handsomely decorated, each in a different style. There are several bright, sunny lounges, and candlelit dinner is served in an oak-panelled dining room, open to non-residents. The five-course table d'hôte menu includes English and French dishes. Fresh seafood is a speciality, with oysters and lobster - choose your own from a tank - menu regulars. In summer a Sunday buffet lunch is served around the pool (heated from May to September) and offers very good value. Last orders: lunch 2pm; dinner 9.30pm.

WHERE TO EAT

Looe
✗ ✉ £££ ⚹

Le Bistro, *Higher Market Street,
East Looe*
Tel: 0503 264152
Open all year
The bare stone walls decorated with
nautical artefacts make this an atmospheric place for dinner in the heart of
old East Looe. The setting is matched
by the cooking, especially the imaginative seafood sauces. The owners,
Ian and Tracy Holmes, moved to
Looe from Kenya two years ago and
have introduced some of their
favourite dishes from East Africa.
The fish and seafood is bought direct
from the fishermen in Looe; red
snapper, kingfish and emperor fish
come from the Middle East. Lighter
pasta-based meals are also served at
lunchtimes. Especially good value is
the fresh lobster, served grilled or in
a Zanzibar sauce, a blend of spices,
coconut and cream. Last orders:
lunch 2pm; dinner 10pm (earlier in
winter).

Looe
✗ ▭ ££ ⚹

The Loft and Cellar Wine Bar, *Quay
Street, East Looe*
Tel: 0503 262131
*Cellar open all year; Loft open for dinner
Easter-end Oct, weekends only in winter*
Occupying one of the oldest build-
ings in Looe which dates back to the
16th century, the wine bar is a cosy

beamed place serving a wide variety
of dishes, from fresh mussels and
scallops to beef vindaloo and grilled
steaks. Upstairs, the more formal Loft
restaurant has a good reputation for
its wide range of local fish and
seafood bought direct from the market. Last orders: lunch 2pm; dinner
10pm.

Polperro
✗ ▭ £££ ⚹

The Kitchen, *Polperro*
Tel: 0503 72780
*Dinner only: closed Tues and open week-
ends only Nov-Easter*
This low red-and-white restaurant on
the road down to the harbour is the
best place to eat in Polperro. Chef Ian
Bateson often greets guests personal-
ly in his small cosy dining room.
There are three main course menus
to choose from: the Kitchen menu
may include crab Dijonnaise or
chicken tikka in a spicy coconut
sauce; the Lobster menu offers lobster in filo pastry or with a Vermouth
and sorrel sauce; and there's an
imaginative vegetarian menu which
may include brazil and cashew nut
loaf or spinach roulade with cheese
and almond filling. Last orders
9.30pm, but phone ahead to check
outside high season.

THE RIVER FOWEY AND CHINA CLAY COUNTRY

The Fowey estuary is one of the most beautiful places in Cornwall, cutting deep into the surrounding hills, and its wooded tidal creeks are easily explored by boat or on foot. The town of Fowey itself is a happy combination of resort and working port and the start of a scenic walk which was popular as far back as Elizabethan times. Around the headland is Menabilly, Daphne du Maurier's famous Cornish home which, although not open to the public, can be spied from the coastal path. Mevagissey is another classic Cornish fishing port, very much given over to tourism, but it lies at the start of a beautiful coast drive past some of the best beaches in the area.

If the weather turns sour head for Lanhydrock House, a National Trust property which vividly evokes life above and below stairs in Victorian times. To the south-west lies china clay country, a land of grey and white slurry hills and deep water-filled pits which give the landscape an eerie, lunar quality. At the Wheal Martyn Museum, north of St Austell, you can learn all about the importance of china clay by touring an old works. There is not a great deal of organised entertainment for children in this area, but there are plenty of opportunities to mess about in boats and swim from safe sandy beaches.

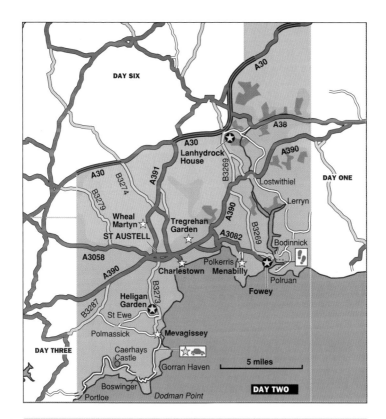

 ## ☆ CHARLESTOWN

In complete contrast to the archetypal Cornish port, Charlestown was the creation of one man, local industrialist Charles Rashleigh who built it between 1791 and 1810. The tree-lined main street leading down to the port is unusually broad and flat, designed so that laden horse-drawn carts could travel three abreast in both directions. In Victorian times it was a busy pilchard and china clay port with a thriving local community. But today it is a quiet place with the feel of a model village, Georgian style, and its period charm makes it a popular location for film and television dramas such as *Poldark* and *The Onedin Line*. From the outer harbour walls there are lovely views over a long stretch of coast and, although there is little shipping now, there are usually some craft in port, shut in by lock gates.

The harbour at Charlestown

Beside the harbour is the **Shipwreck and Heritage Centre**, which contains a good collection of photographs showing how busy Charlestown was early this century. There are displays on the history of diving and the importance of the pilchard catch, but the centre's most interesting exhibits are photographs of shipwrecks in the area: large sailing ships left high and dry, and the fate of a ship which ran aground in Portloe in 1905 and became a pile of smashed wood within 15 minutes. Artefacts salvaged from these wrecks are also exhibited here including pieces of porcelain from the famous Nanking cargo which went down in 1749. Its cargo of Chinese porcelain was salvaged in 1984 and fetched 30 million guilders at Sotheby's in Amsterdam. There's a Heritage Quiz for children: ask for a copy at the entrance.

The Charlestown Shipwreck and Heritage Centre, The Quay. Tel: 0726 69969
Opening times: daily Apr 1-Oct 31, 10am-4pm (later in high season)
Admission: adult £2; child £1.25

A visit to the **Cornish Smoked Fish Company** on Charlestown quay is a must for gourmets. Its shop sells all kinds of smoked fish: sea-farmed rainbow trout, salmon, eels, mussels and its speciality, hot or cold smoked mackerel. Smoked chicken and duck breast are also available. Shop open Mon-Fri 8am-noon, 1.30-5pm all year; Sat 10am-noon Whitsun-end Sept only. Tel: 0726 72356.

FOWEY

Sheltered in a beautiful natural harbour, Fowey (pronounced 'Foy') has a seductive, hedonistic quality. Trading, rather than fishing, has always been its main business, and encounters with foreign lands and peoples through the ages have brought both prosperity and an air of sophistication to the town. Fowey has always attracted opportunist adventurers, keen to make their names and fortunes or, like the Fowey Gallants of the Middle Ages, to display their command of the seas by mischievously raiding small ports along the French and Spanish coasts. In 1380 a Spanish fleet raided Fowey in retaliation, after which two square blockhouses were built on either side of the harbour entrance with a great chain stretched between them. Their remains can still be seen.

Daphne du Maurier's home, Ferryside, viewed from Fowey
(see Walk on p 29)

Until Victorian times, Fowey was an important source of men and ships in time of war and, during the Second World War, American forces sailed from here to Normandy. Today, although its naval role is over, ships from all over the world still arrive to load china clay from the dock upstream of the town. And in summer the estuary fills with thousands of yachts and sailboards, as Fowey dons its summer hat and, in its refined way, entertains holidaymakers who return year after year. The Fowey Royal Regatta is the big event of the summer and takes place in the third week of August, beginning on a Sunday. Fowey's Grand Carnival Parade, entered into with great enthusiasm by the local community, is on the Wednesday evening of regatta week.

Do not attempt to drive through the town's narrow twisting streets. Visitors should park at one of several large car parks signposted on the way in, from where it is a 5-minute walk to the quayside. The **Tourist Information Centre** is located at the Post Office on Custom House Hill (open all year; tel: 0726 833616). Many of the former homes of Fowey's gentry and merchants, a mélange of Elizabethan, Georgian and Victorian styles, have been turned into inns and shops, but the air of comfortable prosperity remains. There is little in the way of souvenirs, instead the shops along Fore Street cater mainly to yachties, divers and surfers. Book Ends (open Mon-Sat) has an excellent selection of new and secondhand books on Cornwall, as well as novels by local authors such as Daphne du Maurier and Sir Arthur Quiller-Couch.

> **Crumbs** on North Street is a good place for lunch. It occupies part of a gift shop and serves delicious home-made food - deep pan pizza, lasagne and fisherman's pie - at a handful of tables. You can also pop in for a Roskilly Farm ice-cream (see Day Four), the best in Cornwall.

There are few specific attractions in Fowey; like so many Cornish ports it is a place of simple pleasures rather than of organised entertainment. However, the old Town Hall contains **Fowey Museum**, a collection of artefacts and old photographs illustrating the history of Fowey. Across the way, the **Aquarium** contains specimens of the diverse sealife found in the estuary and coastal waters: spider crabs, octopus, 60lb conger eels, and thornback rays, as well as the more common sole, plaice and bass. Both attractions are open daily from Easter to the end of September.

The historic town centre of Fowey

Bodinnick Ferry, Fowey

Boat trips operate from the Town Quay, usually from mid-April to the end of September. The 45-minute trip upstream to Golant passes Fowey Docks which you can only really see from the water. During spring tides there are often longer trips up to Lerryn; the evening trips (July and August only) to the Ship at Lerryn, a freehouse which serves good home-made fare, are also very popular. You can also hire a motor-boat, seating up to 5 people, for £5 an hour and explore the estuary on your own.

A very popular diversion for visitors is simply to relax on a quayside bench beside the Bodinnick car ferry and the slipway. This affords much amusement as the ferrymen take a perverse pleasure in humiliating amateur sailors who get in their way. It is also a good spot for watching the river traffic wend its way upstream through delightful scenery which is best appreciated by boat or on foot. The car ferry runs all year from daylight to dusk or 8.45pm, whichever is earlier.

THE HALL WALK

This 4-mile circular walk from Fowey to Polruan has been popular for centuries. In his *Survey of Cornwall* published in 1602,
Richard Carew writes of it as 'a place of diversified pleasings'
with seats for walkers and 'summer houses for their more private retreat and recreation'. It is a fairly easy walk with constantly changing views over the estuary and is best done in the
morning. The path can sometimes be a little muddy, so wear
stout shoes. Outside the summer months you can usually park
in the car park beside the Bodinnick Ferry in Fowey.

Take the car ferry across the river. The house on the right-hand
side of the Bodinnick slipway is Ferryside, Daphne du Maurier's
first home in Cornwall and where she wrote her first novel, *The
Loving Spirit*, set in Plyn, a thinly-disguised Polruan. Walk up
the lane past the Old Ferry Inn and take a footpath marked Hall
Walk on the right. The path skirts the hillside about 150ft above
the river and as you walk around there are constantly changing
perspectives of Fowey, Polruan and the harbour mouth. A
plaque records how in August 1644 King Charles I narrowly
escaped death when a shot intended for him killed a fisherman
instead. The path leaves the main estuary here and passes
through woods, carpeted with bluebells in late April, along Pont
Pill creek where you may see herons fishing at low tide. At the
head of the creek is a small quay with old warehouses and lime
kilns.

Cross the river and head up the hill beside a stream. (If you go
straight on, crossing the lane and heading up the hill you reach
the church of St Wyllow in Lanteglos where Daphne du Maurier
was married. This will add 30 minutes to the 2-hour walk.) The
main path winds back around the creek with benches at inter-
vals so you can sit and admire the view. Finally you reach the
village of Polruan and wend your way down steep steps
between houses to the harbour. For a drink and a snack with the

locals, head for the Russell Inn which has a cosy beamed bar,
good sandwiches, home-made pasties and fresh fish. The
Polruan passenger ferry to White House Quay in Fowey leaves
every 15 minutes, from 7am-11pm.

❂ HELIGAN GARDEN

The rediscovery of Heligan Garden is, in gardening terms, as
important as the unearthing of Pompeii was to Roman history.
One of the finest Victorian gardens in Britain, its pleasure

gardens, walled kitchen gardens and exotic woodlands were tended by 44 gardeners until 1914. During the war the Tremaynes' family home became a hospital for shell victims and they moved to another estate, never to return. It seemed as though the gardens were lost for ever until Tim Smit, archaeologist turned record producer and composer, arrived with a mission to restore them.

In 1991, as work began clearing 10ft-high brambles, hundreds of fallen trees and deep loam, a treasure-house of rare plants and magnificent specimens of exotics was gradually revealed. The gardens are magical and mysterious, and full of interest for gardeners and non-gardeners alike. The northern gardens were designed as pleasure gardens in the 'picturesque' style of the early 19th century with grottoes, wishing wells and rockeries. They contain huge examples, possibly the largest in the world, of rhododendrons collected by Sir Joseph Hooker in the Himalayas during the 1840s (his trip was partly sponsored by the Tremaynes) and varieties of Japonica camellias which are unnamed. Early May is the best time to see these exotics in flower.

The Jungle at Heligan Garden

But at Heligan there is interest throughout the year: the rockery, built to resemble an Alpine mountain pass, with a waterfall and mossy rocks, has been turned into a fernery; the walled kitchen gardens with their ingenious underfloor heating for growing pineapples, as well as melons, grapes, and even kiwi fruit, are being restored to grow these exotic fruits once again. From the foot of the pleasure gardens there are fine views over the coast as far as Fowey. A path leads across a field to what's known as The Jungle. It is the nearest you get in Britain to a tropical rainforest; the air is close and wet, the light dim, and a narrow path winds down a cleft of a valley filled with bamboo, massive tree ferns, palms and much else. You almost expect to hear the hoot of monkeys in the trees above. An experience not to be missed.

Heligan Garden, turn right off the B3273 St Austell-Mevagissey road at the Gorran Haven turning. Tel: 0726 843023
Opening times: daily all year 10.30am-4.30pm (last entry)
Admission: adult £2.40; child 5-16 £1.50

LANHYDROCK HOUSE

One of the grandest houses in Cornwall, Lanhydrock stands at the heart of an impressive park, surrounded by the estate's beech, pine and oak plantations which lead down to the River Fowey. Despite its size, it is not an ostentatious place full of great art and furniture but, like the Robartes family who lived here until 1969, it has an air of solid respectability. The original house was built in the 1630s by Sir Richard Robartes, a Truro tin and wood merchant, in a baronial style with mullioned windows and battlements which completely ignored the arrival of the Renaissance in England. In 1881 a great fire burned down all but the gallery wing, but within three years the house was rebuilt with carving, panelling and plasterwork of the highest quality.

What makes Lanhydrock a particularly interesting place to visit is its vivid evocation of High Victorian ideals: the careful segregation of public and private, male and female, master and servant. It remained virtually unchanged in the 20th century as Gerald Agar-Robartes and his unmarried sisters Violet and Everilda, all born in the 1880s, lived here until the Sixties, preserving the Victorian timewarp and donating the house, its contents and the park to the National Trust.

As you tour the house you get a very clear picture of life above and below stairs. The attention to detail is so complete that you feel that the family and servants have simply stepped out for a while. In Miss Eva's boudoir, the table is laid for tea, complete with a sponge cake baked by one of the curators. In the bedrooms the dressing tables are cluttered with bits of lace, hairpins and brooches; the housemaids' closet contains four sets of equipment - rectangular buckets holding dusters, brushes and tins of Zebo for blackleading grates; the luggage room is piled high with dome-topped trunks, hat boxes and a wheelchair, and the Ladies' Dresses room contains a large selection of Edwardian clothes worn by Lady Robartes. The family obviously never threw anything away and this collection of household paraphernalia brings the place to life in a way that the heavy Victorian furniture and family portraits never could.

You wander around at your own pace - a good free guide to the function and contents of the rooms is available in the Hall - and there are stewards on hand to answer any questions. The extensive servants' quarters are a highlight of the tour, untouched since Edwardian times, and containing every conceivable labour-saving device. In the kitchen an elaborate mechanical spit could roast joints and game together over the open fire. There is a scullery, bake house, larders of all kinds, and a dairy, all with their original contents laid out just as if work was about to start.

Another highlight is the Gallery, the only part of the house to escape the fire of 1881. This was fortunate as it has always been regarded as the finest room at Lanhydrock because of its magnificent 17th-century plaster ceiling depicting Old Testament scenes, most notably the stories of Adam and Eve and Noah's Ark. Below, entered from the front courtyard, is a small museum containing family mementos, even down to old dance cards, and contemporary photographs and newspaper cuttings of the fire.

Behind the house is a small 15th-century church, built by the Augustinian Priory which formerly owned the land. A large walled garden, laid out originally in the 1860s, rises up behind. It is known for its many species of magnolia, at their best in April, and is a pleasant place for a stroll if you do not have time for a longer walk down to the River Fowey. The river can be reached along the half-mile avenue of sycamores, originally planted in 1648, and now supplemented with beech.

The Kitchen at Lanhydrock House

There are two places to eat lunch: the old housekeeper's sitting room serves simple salads, quiches, and jacket potatoes; the former servants' hall more substantial home-made fare, wine and beer between noon and 2.15pm, and cream teas from 3-5pm. Children may take a greater interest in the house if they have a copy of the special children's guide, Look at Lanhydrock, on sale in the bookshop at the entrance to the park.

Lanhydrock House, follow signposts from A38 Bodmin-Liskeard or B3268 Bodmin-Lostwithiel roads. Tel: 0208 73320

Opening times: House - daily Apr 1-Oct 31, 11am-5.30 pm except Mon unless a Bank Hol; garden and grounds - open dawn to dusk all year

Admission: adult £5.20; child £2.60; NT members free

MENABILLY

If you turn right off the A3082 Par-Fowey road, signposted Polkerris, a lane leads to Menabilly, an estate owned by the Rashleigh family, but leased to Daphne du Maurier for many years. The reputedly haunted house and its location were the inspiration for the fictional Manderley in *Rebecca* and the setting for *The King's General*. The house is not open to the public, and you can only see the back of it from the road, or survey the estate by taking a walk. Park in the car park in a field belonging to Menabilly Barton farm and walk down past the farmhouse towards the sea.

The path has been hewn out of the rock and descends to Polridmouth Cove (pronounced 'Pridmouth'), a popular swimming place for locals from Fowey. There are two small beaches of pale sand, the most attractive lies at the foot of a series of small lakes surrounded by a beautiful lawn which mark the seaward side of Menabilly. However, for a view of the house which Daphne du Maurier loved so much and was unceremoniously ousted from when the lease expired, you will need to turn right at the first beach and follow the coastal footpath for half-a-mile to the top of the beacon at Gribbin Head, from where you can survey the Menabilly estate.

MEVAGISSEY

This is regarded as one of Cornwall's most picturesque fishing ports: brightly painted clapboard and slate-fronted houses line the quaysides, and the hills behind are refreshingly free of modern development. However, there have been some unforgivable concessions to tourism which detract from its charm: fish and chip shops (the fish from Greenland), plasticky modern pubs and cafeterias, an amusement arcade on the quay, and shops full of cheap souvenirs made in the Far East. It is best avoided in high summer when the hordes descend, but in the early evening and out of season it is a very pleasant place for a stroll.

Its focus is the unusual inner and outer harbours, the former rebuilt in the 18th century, along with all the quays, piers, fish cellars, warehouses and many of the cottages. Huge quantities of pilchards used to be caught in the waters off Mevagissey and landed here where they were cured in rock salt, packed in barrels and sent off to Italy and the West Indies. Today it is still an important fishing port, with a substantial fleet of trawlers and smaller boats, and you can sit on the quay and watch their comings-and-goings. Like many fishing ports, it has a small sea aquarium with examples of the types of fish found in local waters.

Mevagissey

A good place for lunch is **Mr Bistro**, a simple restaurant with pine furnishings to the left of the quay. The fish and seafood served here really is fresh - not always the case in Cornish ports - and includes scallops, prawns, crab claws, mussels, oysters and whelks. Open for lunch and dinner daily Easter-end October; tel: 0726 842432.

The **Mevagissey Museum**, housed in a former boatbuilder's workshop at the far end of the left quay, tells the history of Mevagissey with the help of hundreds of photographs, copied from originals owned by the local people. There are all sorts of folksy artefacts collected in the area, from a two-man lathe to old gowns, a granite apple crusher and some of the strange things found in local fishermen's nets.

Mevagissey Museum. Tel: 0726 843568
Opening times: Good Fri-Whitsun daily 2-4pm; Whitsun-end Sept daily 11am-5pm
Admission: adult 30p; child 10p

Behind the main shopping street is the **World of Model Railways**, a must for the enthusiast. Created by Arthur Howeson and opened to the public 22 years ago, its centrepiece is a giant landscaped lay-out where 50 trains, controlled in automatic sequence, run through beautifully detailed scenery, from the Alps with moving skiers and cable cars to Cornwall's china clay country. Around the walls are over 2,000 models illustrating the history of model railways, with British, European and American model trains. Many date from the 1920s and '30s, the days of the Great Western, LNER, Southern and LNS railways. There is also a shop selling modern model trains and kits to construct your own scenery.

World of Model Railways, Meadow Street. Tel: 0726 842457
Opening times: Easter and Whitsun-end Oct, daily 11am-5pm, although afternoons only if slack; Nov-Easter, Sun only 2-4pm
Admission: adult £1.95; child £1.45

> The landscape inland of Mevagissey is particularly lovely in a quiet rural way. Head for **St Ewe**, a sleepy timeless village which has a fine church and a good pub with a garden called The Crown (see Where to Eat). In **Polmassick**, the next village, there is a vineyard where you can taste and buy Cornish wines. It is open to the public daily from June-end September 11am-5pm, except Monday.

☆ MEVAGISSEY-PORTLOE DRIVE

This is a wonderful scenic route around an unspoilt part of the south coast which gives the feel of old Cornwall, before the bungalows and caravans arrived to occupy so many beautiful headlands. As the roads are single-track lanes which climb steep hills with hairpin turns, this is not a drive to be attempted in August or with a heavily loaded car.

From Mevagissey, head west or right out of the port up on to a headland from where there are magnificent views over the coast. After a couple of miles the road forks; take the left fork to Trewollock and left again to Gorran Haven, threading down through the village to the beach and the church. Turn right here and head up a steep hill to Lamledra Farm from where there are fabulous views over Dodman Point. As you leave the coast, turn left to Penare and then right to **Hemmick Beach**, a delightful small sandy bay with a car park.

Pass through Boswinger, turn left at the T-junction for Tregavarras and follow the road as it winds down to Porthluney Cove and **Caerhays Castle,** a castellated mansion designed by John Nash, architect of Buckingham Palace. Beautifully situated between two headlands, its woodland garden, designed by J C Williams, a leading British plantsman who owned Caerhays at the turn of the century, is considered one of Cornwall's finest. It contains one of the richest collections of Asiatic trees and shrubs in Britain. The gardens are usually opened to the public during April and May: Monday-Friday 11am-4.30pm.

> With the Castle as its backdrop, **Porthluney Beach** is an excellent place for sunbathing or a picnic, either on the grassy areas behind or on the broad sandy beach itself. It is also a reasonably safe place for children to swim, and at low tide there is plenty of room for beach games. There is a large car park with toilets and a refreshment kiosk in season.

From Porthluney Cove the road climbs a steep hill through magnificent woodlands which in autumn are so full of pheasants that you risk running them over. After a mile or so there is a switchback left turn, signposted Portholland. Take this road and drive back to the coast to East and West Portholland, two tiny hamlets of estate cottages where time has stood still. The road continues, if you take two further left turns to the unspoilt fishing hamlet of Portloe where you can enjoy a drink or a meal at The Lugger Hotel (see Where to Stay) overlooking the sea.

☆ TREGREHAN GARDEN

The 20-acre garden at Tregrehan (pronounced 'Trgrain') is worth seeing if you are a keen gardener, and is of particular interest to lovers of camellias and exotic conifers. The woodland garden

Veteran rhododendrons in Tregrehan Garden

was created in the early 19th century when William Carlyon began planting varieties of trees brought back from North America and Japan, notably Douglas fir and Japanese cedar. The work was carried on by his descendants, but the garden suffered from neglect after the Second World War and there is now a lot of new planting being done.

It is particularly interesting to visit in late March and early April when the camellias and some venerable old rhododendrons, the size of trees, are in flower. Later in April the Bluebell Wood is at its finest. Among the garden's other attractions are conifers and pines from all over the world, some the largest of their kind grown in Britain, and an eerie avenue of Irish yews. In September, the glasshouses are at their best, filled especially with *lapagerias* from Chile in all shades of red, pink and white.

Tregrehan Garden, entrance on the A390 St Blazey-St Austell road
Opening times: mid-Mar - end June and Sept, Wednes-Sun 10.30am-5pm
Admission: adult £2; child 75p

> The **Mid-Cornwall Galleries**, on the A390 close to Tregrehan Garden, occupy an old school and display a good selection of quality craftwork by local artists: ceramics, glass, woodwork, jewellery and original watercolours and etchings. The exhibitions change regularly, and all the items are for sale. Open Monday-Saturday 10am-5pm all year.

 ## WHEAL MARTYN

A wide area all around St Austell is mined for china clay, the waste tips creating an almost fantastical landscape which has a strange, eerie beauty. Among the vibrant green patchwork of fields and woods, the land suddenly erupts into white pyramids and long fluted barrows and then falls away into deep pits, some filled with milky green or blue water. The place to find out more about this important Cornish industry is the Wheal Martyn China Clay Museum ('wheal' is Cornish for workings) on a site where china clay was processed from the 1820s. The self-guided historical tour is well conceived and educational, and includes an interesting nature walk into the heart of this almost lunar landscape. If you follow both the history and nature trails you need to allow two hours for a visit.

Start your visit by viewing the 10-minute video film on the history of china clay and how it was 'won'. For centuries, the Chinese had jealously guarded the secret of making high-quality porcelain from Kaolin (their name for china clay, a form of decomposed granite), and it was not until the mid-18th century that Europeans learned the secret of the process and found, under Cornish soil, the largest and best quality deposits of china clay in the world. After the film you walk outside and follow a trail around the different stages of the refining process, as it was in the 1930s when Wheal Martyn closed down.

China clay pits viewed from Wheal Martyn

The water wheels, used for pumping the clay slurry around the works, still turn although the pits have been colonised by bullrushes, frogs and newts. Information boards contain good explanations of each part of the sifting process which relied on gravity to separate the clay from the sand and mica. In the drying sheds there is an exhibition of early pieces of European porcelain, and old photographs of the works in action, as well a look at the china clay production process today.

The second part of the tour is a nature trail up to the modern workings. At the start there is a small children's play area with swings and climbing frames set in sand. Rhododendrons thrive on the slurry mountains and have spread like weeds, turning the conical white hills green. Walk to the top for the best views and a plaque identifying landmarks. You can climb higher still, following a works road, to a pit viewing point. Far below men scurry like ants playing with Tonka toys to win the precious clay. While on the surface small white cottages await their fate on narrowing strips of green amid this vast silver-grey landscape.

For a closer look, you can join a **one-day china clay country tour** using your own car, led by an experienced guide. The tours depart on Tuesdays and Wednesdays in summer and take in many places not normally accessible to visitors. Book in advance by contacting the Museum.

The reception building itself contains a café serving home-made soups, lasagne and jacket potatoes, and a large selection of books on all aspects of Cornwall, from novels and memoirs to serious history and archaeology books. Guides to the history and nature trails are on sale, but they are not really necessary as the explanations are clear and comprehensive.

Wheal Martyn China Clay Museum, on the A391 near Carthew, north of St Austell.
Tel: 0726 850362
Opening times: daily Mar 29-Oct 31, 10am-6pm (last admission 5pm)
Admission: adult £3.60; child £1.80

WHERE TO STAY

Bodinnick
🏠 🐾 🛏 ££ ✗

The Old Ferry Inn, *Bodinnick,*
Polruan PL23 1LX
Tel: 0726 870237
Open all year
This 17th-century inn stands on a steep hill above the River Fowey. There are 12 cosy bedrooms and those at the front have lovely views across the river. The car ferry stops running at dusk, but you can catch the passenger ferry from Polruan, a short drive away, to spend the evening in Fowey itself. However, the three snug bars, their walls full of bric-a-brac, are welcoming places to spend the evening, and there's a games room at the back. Good simple bar food, and more substantial evening meals served in the dining room. Last orders: lunch 2pm; dinner in restaurant 8.15pm.

Fowey
🏠 🛏 ££ ✗

Carnethic House, *Lambs Barn, Fowey*
PL23 1HQ
Tel: 0726 833336
Open Feb-Nov
This lovely Regency house stands in beautiful gardens whose immaculate lawns, with putting green and grass tennis court, are the pride and joy of owner David Hogg and his wife Trisha. It is a superbly run place with

the feel of a welcoming country home. First-floor rooms at the front have distant estuary views and are pleasantly furnished. Downstairs, there is a light, airy sitting room and bar opening on to the garden. Guests are introduced to each other over a drink before dinner which makes for an intimate house party feel. The four-course set menu (two choices for each course) may include home-made soup or smoked mackerel, local scallops in butter and lemon or steak, chocolate roulade or apple and passion fruit pie, and a cheese board. The cooking is excellent, based on fresh local produce. Small wine list. There is a heated swimming pool in the garden. Early booking advised.

Fowey

🏠 ✕ 🛏 🚆 ££ 🕴

Marina Hotel, *Esplanade, Fowey PL23 1HY*
Tel: 0726 833315
Open Mar 1-Oct 31
This two-star hotel occupies an elegant Georgian building right on the waterfront. Seven of the bright, tastefully decorated bedrooms have views over the river, and four of these have balconies which give access to the small quayside garden. The Waterside Restaurant serves dinner and has similar expansive river views. The one drawback is the lack of a car park; guests must unload luggage quickly outside and then park in the town car park. Courtesy transport back to your car is arranged when checking out. Last orders for dinner 8.30pm.

Lanhydrock

🔄 ✉ £ 🕴3

Treffrey Farm, *Lanhydrock, Bodmin PL30 5AF*
Tel: 0208 82272
Open Easter-end Oct
On the edge of the Lanhydrock estate, this is a beautiful listed Georgian farmhouse on a dairy farm with a slate-tiled front and a fine panelled sitting room. There are three handsome bedrooms, one with a four-poster, and all with their own bathrooms. Owner Pat Smith is a mine of information on the area. Traditional farmhouse cooking based on fresh produce including vegetables from the garden. Outside there is a small children's playground next to some superbly furnished and equipped self-catering cottages, converted from former stone barns.

Mevagissey

🔄 ✉ £ 🕴5

Kerryanna Country Guest House, *Treleaven Farm, Mevagissey PL26 6RZ*
Tel: 0726 843558
Open Easter-end Oct
An attractive modern farmhouse at the head of a valley leading down to the sea, it has been purpose-built for taking in guests and, with its large sunny sitting room and licensed bar, it has more the feel of a guesthouse. The six bedrooms are bright, spotless and decorated in a simple tasteful way. All have en suite shower rooms. The gardens include a putting green and a 40ft heated swimming pool. Traditional home cooking six nights a week.

Portloe

⌂ ✕ ▭ £££ ✻12

The Lugger Hotel, *Portloe, Truro*
TR2 5RD
Tel: 0872 501322
Open Feb-Nov

At the heart of an unspoilt fishing hamlet stands this rambling white-washed hotel, dating back to the 17th century. The public rooms with their beamed ceilings and comfortable seating manage to be both bright and cosy. Bedrooms are prettily decorat-ed, some with antiques; those in the new wing are more spacious but less characterful. The dining room over-looks a tiny beach, and in fine weath-er bar lunches are served on slate-flagged terraces above the bay. The restaurant has a good reputation, using fresh local produce where pos-sible, especially fish and seafood. Non-residents should reserve ahead. Last orders: bar lunches 2.15pm; dinner 8.30pm.

WHERE TO EAT

Fowey

✕ ▭ £££ ✻

Food for Thought, *The Quay, Fowey*
Tel: 0726 832221
Dinner only; closed Jan and Sun

In a lovely old building on the Town Quay, this intimate restaurant with its smart rustic interior serves some of the best food in Fowey. Fresh fish and seafood are specialities - ravioli of crab meat, whole Dover sole cooked in the oven with shellfish and a herb crust, scallops in garlic butter - but there is a selection of meat dishes including Scottish rib steak and baby quails. Last orders 9.30pm.

Polkerris

☞ ▭ £ ✻

The Rashleigh Inn, *Polkerris*
Tel: 0726 813991
Open all year; à la carte restaurant
Wednes-Sat

The panelled bar of this pleasant waterside pub is lined with old pho-tographs of Polkerris, once an impor-tant pilchard curing centre. In fine weather, tables are set out on the ter-race above the small beach which overlooks St Austell Bay and is a great place to watch the sun set. The bar menu is extensive but the food appears to be home-made and may include rabbit and bacon pie and chilli with rice, and a good selection of vegetarian dishes. Part of the inn has been turned into a more formal restaurant serving French-inspired dishes (reserve ahead), but the bar menu offers better value. Last orders for bar meals: lunch 2.30pm (Sun 2pm); dinner 10pm.

St Ewe

☞ ⊀ ✉ £ ✻

The Crown, *St Ewe, near Mevagissey*
Tel: 0726 843322
Open all year

With its flagstone floor, roaring log fire and sturdy wooden furnishings, this is a quintessential country pub in a lovely village. The food matches the setting: good pasties, local crab salad, fish of the day, steaks and home-made puddings. You can eat either in the bar or in the restaurant where children are welcome. Tables in the rear garden in summer. Last orders: lunch 2.30pm (Sun 2pm); dinner 9.30pm.

THE ROSELAND
PENINSULA, TRURO
AND ST AGNES

When the north coast lies under a granite sky, the sheltered estuary of the River Fal may bask in sunshine; it can also work the other way round. Travelling between the two coasts takes under an hour so you can easily head from showers into sunshine. For those who like their coastline wild and windswept, the north coast around pretty St Agnes has a rugged beauty. Scattered over the cliffs are the ruins of tin and copper mines which once brought the area such prosperity, and the Poldark Mine is a chance to see what life must have been like for Victorian tinners working underground. Young children will enjoy the St Agnes Leisure Park and the shire horse farm nearby.

However, if you prefer lush sheltered valleys and gentle contours, head for the soft underbelly of Cornwall: the estuary of the Fal and the Roseland peninsula. Here the Gulf Stream creates the moist, mild conditions favoured by plants from much warmer climes: the gardens at Trelissick and Trewithen are two of the finest in Cornwall. The sheltered creeks of the Fal estuary are best explored by boat and in summer there are frequent excursions from Truro, Falmouth and St Mawes. On a really rotten day, retreat to Truro, the attractive Georgian county town which has the best shopping in Cornwall.

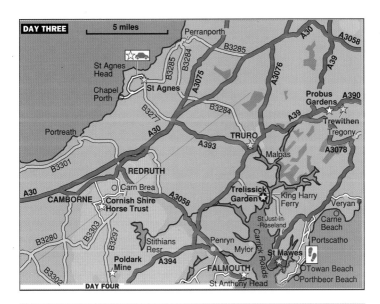

THE CORNISH SHIRE HORSE TRUST

In a rural valley full of abandoned tin mines, this small farm is the home of 21 shire horses, including five endangered Suffolk shires. You are taken around and introduced to each of the horses in turn, told their life story, and allowed to stroke them. Sometimes you will see the shires at work on the farm, ploughing or pulling loads, and on most days visitors are taken on wagon rides. In one of the large barns, there is an impressive collection of carriages and carts in fine condition, among them a landau, game cart, pony chaise and a Victorian horse omnibus which plied for hire between Falmouth and St Just and brought the mail. The wheelwright and blacksmith on the farm still undertake work and you are welcome to watch them in action. It is a friendly, informal place where you are very welcome to muck in and help out on the farm for a day. Cream teas are available.

The Cornish Shire Horse Trust, Lower Gryllis, Treskillard (from the B3297 Redruth-Helston road turn right at Four Lanes crossroads then first left after the Countryman pub). Tel: 0209 713606
Opening times: Easter-end Sept, daily except Sat 10am-6pm
Admission: adult £2.75; child £1.50

Wagon rides at the Cornish Shire Horse Trust

From the Shire Horse Trust it is a couple of miles to **Carn Brea** (take the road to Carnkie beside the Countryman pub and then second left up a track to the top of the hill). This small moor, covered in flowering heather and gorse in September, stands 750ft above sea level and from the top of the granite tor there are panoramic views over the north coast and across a rural landscape peppered with chimneys and tumbledown stone mine buildings, the relics of Cornwall's industrial past. The tiny castle, a former hunting lodge, is now a restaurant (see Where to Eat).

☆   FALMOUTH

Falmouth markets itself as 'the resort which has everything'. It is certainly beautifully situated in the largest of Cornwall's deep water estuaries, here called Carrick Roads, but it is not really a holiday resort. In the shopping streets people go about with a sense of purpose, and the town's focus is still the port, busy with shipping as well as pleasure craft. Although there are good sandy beaches on the south side of the town, there are far more appealing places to relax and cleaner places to swim in this area. Parking in the town centre is difficult and in high summer it is tempting to give Falmouth a miss and survey the town and its harbour from St Mawes or St Anthony Head (see walk panel) instead.

Falmouth's importance lies in the past when it provided a crucial link between Britain and the rest of the world. Chosen in 1688 as Britain's chief port for the despatch of mail overseas, its fast Packet ships sailed the world and, together with cargo and passenger ships, made it one of the busiest ports in Britain until steam replaced sail. As you walk along High Street and Market Street which snake around the harbour, hemmed in on the landward side by steep hills, there are reminders of its seafaring past, from the former homes of Victorian Packet Captains to old inns on narrow cobbled alleys where sailors would celebrate a successful voyage. Falmouth's **Tourist Information Centre** is at 28 Killigrew Street, opposite the bus station; tel: 0326 312300.

From Prince of Wales Pier in the town centre, there is a large choice of **boat trips** around the Fal and its tributaries. Regular ferry services run to St Mawes and Flushing all year (except Sundays in winter). Boat excursions take in either the River Fal and its creeks, sailing as far as Malpas for lunch at the Heron Inn (see Where to Eat) and Truro, if tides permit, or south to explore the creeks of the Helford River. Boats leave 10am-5.30pm, Easter to end October. Most trips last two hours, although you can get off in Truro and take a later boat back. You can also hire self-drive motor boats and sailing dinghies from Custom House Quay; telephone 0860 789109 for information and bookings.

Commanding the entrance to Carrick Roads is **Pendennis Castle**, the largest and best preserved of the Cornish forts built by Henry VIII. What makes it especially worth a visit is the imaginative way in which English Heritage has brought the castle to life. Inside the keep waxwork figures in Tudor dress man the cannons and a commentary recreates the fury of battle, the struggle to prime and fire the cannons (with smoke effects), and the dangers faced by the soldiers. There is also a video narrated by a fictional Master of the Guns on life in the fort.

The Governor's apartments contain modern furnishings by local craftsmen in vernacular style to indicate their original function and give a sense of scale. The whole project is very well conceived, and children will be impressed by the bangs and the smoke. A massive curtain wall, built in Elizabethan times, surrounds the fort itself and proved so strong that it enabled 900 men to withstand a five-month siege during the Civil War. Today it is an excellent place to relax and watch the large number of ships, yachts and fishing boats enter Carrick Roads.

Pendennis Castle, Castle Drive (parking inside the walls). Tel: 0326 316594
Opening times: Apr 1-Sept 30, daily 10am-6pm; Oct-Mar 10am-4.30pm when closed
Mon and for lunch
Admission: adult £1.80; child over 5 90p

☆ ## POLDARK MINE

Despite the number of abandoned tin mines all over Cornwall, this is the only chance visitors have to go underground since the closing of the more impressive workings at Geevor near Land's End. The Poldark Mine (no relation to the fictional Ross Poldark of Winston Graham's novels) dates back to 1492 when surface tin was mined here. The underground tunnels which visitors enter today belonged to Wheal Roots and were dug by hand in the 18th century. The workings are not large but they are impressive none the less, and more tunnels are being rediscovered.

A film on the history of Cornish tin mining is shown in a small cinema and it's worth seeing this before going down the mine itself. There are three routes, graded according to difficulty, as there are steep narrow staircases to climb and vertigo sufferers should avoid the most difficult route. The low ceilings, dank air and dripping walls make you realise how awful it must have been to spend your working life in a tin mine. Along the way life-size tableaux of hunched miners vividly recreate working conditions, and it is with a sense of relief that you reach the exit half an hour later.

The complex also includes Poldark Village where sets recreate tin miners' and owners' home lives around 1800. Of more interest, especially for the mechanically minded, are the museum chambers which contain dozens of detailed working model engines, often made by miners as a hobby, as well as full-size

Inside Poldark Mine

Models of mine engine houses at St Agnes Leisure Park

steam engines now worked by compressed air. There is also a well laid out collection of mining memorabilia and domestic bygones, including one of the largest collections of laundry irons in the world.

Outside, in the attractive landscaped grounds, there are examples of the great pumping engines which once occupied the tall ruined buildings you see all over this area. And to make sure children don't get bored there is a variety of entertainment for them: bumper boats, a giant slide, and an amusement arcade which you cannot avoid as the exit is through it. There are several eating places, serving uninspiring snacks and larger meals, and you can find a drink in the Miners Arms, although you may prefer to head for a more atmospheric pub. It takes around two hours to see everything. Some parts of the complex are overtly commercial but if you are interested in Cornwall's industrial heritage, the museum and the mine tour make this attraction worth a visit.

The Poldark Mine, Wendron (on the B3297 Helston-Redruth road). Tel: 0326 563166
Opening times: Apr 1-Oct 31, daily 10.30am-5.30pm (last entry 4pm)
Admission: adult £4.95; child £2.75

☆ PROBUS GARDENS

If you are a keen gardener you will not want to miss Probus, a demonstration garden run by the Cornwall Education Committee. Within its seven acres, gardening techniques and tips are put into practice by the experts. You can see the effect of different kinds of weedkillers and fertilisers on lawns, learn how to make your own compost, look at the growth patterns of dwarf conifers and the colours of different kinds of daffodil and narcissus, and discover why solid walls and fences do not provide effective shelter belts for plants. If you are thinking of buying plants in some of the excellent nurseries in this area Probus will show you how they grow under different soil conditions.

Even if you have no garden but have an interest in trees and flowers, Probus is worth a visit. There is an historical garden, arranged in chronological order, with examples of indigenous plants such as Cornish heather and elm, and species introduced by the Romans, French monks and the great plant collectors of the 19th century. In late September, you can taste examples of the traditional English apples and pears that you never see in the greengrocer's now. There are impressive displays of different kinds of clematis, heather and conifers, plants used in traditional dyes, from camomile to woad, and a map of Cornwall laid out on a raised mound showing all the different rocks that make up its geology.

Probus Gardens, 5 miles from Truro on the A390 Truro-St Austell road.
Tel: 0872 74282
Opening times: May-Sept, daily 10am-5pm; Oct-Apr, Mon-Fri 10am-4.30pm
Admission: adult £1.50; children free

☆ ST AGNES

This large handsome village of honey-coloured stone cottages stands at the head of a steep valley winding down to Trevaunance Cove, a pleasant sandy beach which has a lifeguard in season. St Agnes has a strong community feel, and leads a life outside of tourism, which is low-key here. A wander around its lanes is a must for anyone interested in vernacular architecture. The superior quality of the tin mined in this area made St Agnes prosperous, and this is reflected in its well-built homes, from the steep terraces of neat two-up, two-down miners' cottages to the more substantial villas of mine captains, all set in pretty flower gardens.

The **Railway Inn** on Vicarage road, the main street, is a friendly, low-beamed pub, famous for its horse brasses and extensive collection of shoes, from clogs and pattens to Turkish slippers and Chinese pumps. It serves simple home-made fare: soups, sandwiches, pasties and pies, and there is a separate eating area where children are allowed. Open 11am-11pm, but may close on winter afternoons.

A former chapel of rest has been converted into the **St Agnes Museum**, which opened in 1991 and contains an interesting collection of well arranged exhibits covering the history of the area and its folklore. It also contains a small video room where you can watch a series of interesting films covering such subjects as Tin Streaming in Trevellas, the St Agnes Carnival, and a Walking Westward documentary on the coast here. If you are the only visitor, the curator will put on the video of your choice; otherwise they run in sequence.

St Agnes Museum, on the B3277 into St Agnes
Opening times: Easter-end Oct 10am-5pm
Admission: free

Young children will enjoy visiting **St Agnes Leisure Park** whose focus is a model village depicting Cornwall in miniature, a succession of tableaux set in pretty landscaped gardens. The models are exquisitely crafted and include Trerice Manor where Elizabethan music is played in the background, Truro Cathedral, a Victorian mining village, and Wheal Duchy tin mine with its wheel house, crusher and stamps. Afterwards you can visit the Lost World of the Dinosaur, containing models of prehistoric mammoths and cave bears; a haunted house full of skeletons; and moving tableaux depicting fairy tales and nursery rhymes from Red Riding Hood to the old woman who lived in the shoe. These are by no means up to Disney standards, but they seem to delight children under eight.

St Agnes Leisure Park, on the B3277 south of St Agnes. Tel: 0872 552793
Opening times: daily Mar 28-Oct 31, 10am-6pm, last entry 4pm; except Jul 1-Sept 10, last entry 9pm
Admission: adult £4.10; two children under 14 free with each adult

☆ ST AGNES HEAD DRIVE

Turn left off the B3277 just after the museum in St Agnes, sign-posted Chapelporth, to drive along the top of one of the most dramatic cliffscapes in Cornwall. Here the high moorland meets the sea and from the **St Agnes Head**, where the wind will rock your car on a stormy day, there are magnificent views over the north coast. There is plenty of parking space on the cliff top and on a fine summer's day this is a lovely spot for a picnic. A large colony of kittewakes breeds here, as well as herring gulls, ful-mars and guillemots. You may also be lucky enough to see seals on the rocks far below, and the odd harmless basking shark.

Back on Beacon Drive take the next right turn to the old **Wheal Coates** mine, one of over a hundred former tin and copper mines in this area. You can wander around the ruined Victorian engine houses and descend to Towanroath, a former pumping house, perched on a narrow shelf half-way down the cliffside. In September the cliffs are covered in a glorious display of flower-ing dwarf heather, all shades of pink and purple.

At the end of Beacon Drive, turn right down to **Chapel Porth**, where deep rockpools and a fine expanse of sand are left by the retreating tide. There is a large car park, and more excellent walking over the headlands on either side, or you can walk around the base of the cliffs which are pitted with caves. The beach is popular with families in summer, and, as swimming can be dangerous, there is a lifeguard in season.

The **Hedgehog Café** in the car park serves delicious snacks: home-made soup, croque monsieur, imaginative hot sandwich-es, and a calorie-rich Hedgehog special - Cornish ice-cream smothered in clotted cream and roasted hazelnuts. Open daily 11am-5pm April to end September; weekends in October.

☆ ST MAWES

Although 'Ros' really means 'peninsula' in Cornish, the Roseland peninsula is an apt description for this gentle rolling landscape criss-crossed by quiet country lanes which lead even-tually to St Mawes. In spring you pass fields full of cultivated daffodils, and down along the wooded creeksides there is a profusion of wild flowers. St Mawes faces south giving it a pleasant sunny aspect, its white cottages and villas climbing the hillsides behind its busy yachting harbour. There is not much in the way of sights; it is simply a lovely spot to while away a sunny afternoon watching the harbour traffic pass along Carrick Roads.

> There is a large car park which makes St Mawes a good jumping-off point for **boat trips**. The St Mawes Ferry Company (0209 861020) operates a regular passenger service to Falmouth, a 20-minute ride away, all year, except Sundays in winter. From Easter to mid-October there are 2-hour cruises along the Helford River and up the River Fal to Malpas. Departures depend on the tides: telephone 0209 214901 for information.

On the outskirts of St Mawes stands **St Mawes Castle**, a smaller version of Pendennis Castle in Falmouth. It was also built by Henry VIII as a defence against French invasion, at a cost of £5,000. It is well preserved but does not have the atmosphere of Pendennis. Inside there are old photographs of St Mawes and a small collection of 18th-century weapons on loan from the Tower of London. However, its situation is superb. You can picnic on the grass bank inside its curtain wall and watch the yachts and ships enter and leave this beautiful natural harbour.

St Mawes Castle, signposted on the A3078. Tel: 0326 270526
Opening times: Apr 1-Sept 30, daily 10am-6pm; Oct-Mar, 10am-4pm, closed Mon
Admission: adult £1.20; child 5-16 60p

The Church of St Just-in-Roseland

One of the circular cottages in Veryan

From St Mawes it is a short drive, or a lovely two-mile waterside walk, to the church of **St Just-in-Roseland**. The mediaeval church itself is not exceptional, but its location is. It is hard to think of a more beautiful place in which to be buried. The churchyard is a sub-tropical garden with ponds and a waterfall tumbling down to the edge of a creek. Many of the trees and shrubs, which include palms, bamboo, tree ferns and an aromatic box hedge, were planted at the turn of the century. It is a tranquil place to linger, reading the inscriptions on the tombstones and drinking in the beautiful scenery.

The village of **Veryan**, signposted off the A3078 to St Mawes, is one of the most enchanting in the county. Guarding the road which passes through it are two pairs of thatched and white-washed round houses surmounted by crosses. They were built in the early 19th century by a vicar who chose this unusual style to provide no north side for the Devil to enter by and no corners for him to lurk in - although another theory says they were built to protect the village against witches who also cannot abide a house without corners.

ST ANTHONY HEAD WALK

This is a fairly long walk - the whole circuit takes three hours or more - although there are short cuts, but it encompasses a great diversity of scenery, from cliffs and beaches to creeks and woodlands, as well as panoramic views over Falmouth and St Mawes. This walk is best done in the morning with the sun behind you. From the A3078 follow signs to Porthscatho, but do not turn off into the village: go straight on following signs for St Anthony. There is National Trust parking at Porth Farm (in two fields

St Mawes Castle viewed from St Anthony Battery

either side of the farm). From here cross the road and take the footpath to Towan Beach, a particularly lovely sandy strand punctuated by rock pools which is very popular with families in high summer.

Turn right along the coastal footpath which hugs the cliff-top, passing through fields carpeted in wild flowers in early summer. After 15 minutes' walk you reach Porthbeor Beach, a southwest facing beach of fine sand reached down steep slate steps where the swimming is best near high tide. Carry on to the top of the ridge and a great swathe of coast is laid out before you: the Lizard peninsula, the entrance to the Helford River, the lovely sandy bay at Maenporth, Falmouth with its castle and docks and, on the other side of Carrick Roads, St Mawes.

Where the path forks turn left to reach St Anthony Battery, a fully operational artillery fort until 1959 and yet another lovely spot from which to watch the harbour traffic. From here you could head back to Porth Farm along the road, but it's worth persevering and passing through the lower car park to pick up the footpath again. In April white hawthorn blossom cascades down the cliffs like a waterfall as you round the headland to face St Mawes across the water.

From here the path runs alongside the Percuil river before curling around the back of Place House, a Victorian pile hiding a church with a fine Norman doorway and an interior which Nikolaus Pevsner described as 'the best example in the county of what a parish church was like in the 12th and 13th centuries'. Where the footpath meets the lane, you can turn right to take the road back to the car park or, to complete this circular walk, turn left and follow the coastal footpath through woodlands to the head of the creek and Porth Farm up to the right.

✪ TRELISSICK GARDEN

Of all the gardens open to the public in Cornwall, Trelissick is the one which appeals to the widest range of people. Even those with no more than a passing interest in fine gardens will enjoy strolling around its beautiful lawns and woodlands. In sheltered valleys all along the south coast the mild maritime climate and acid soil is perfect for the cultivation of rhododendrons, camellias and magnolias, as well as sub-tropical trees and shrubs. At Trelissick many of the older exotics and trees were planted in the mid-19th century, but the 25-acre garden visitors see today was largely created in the 1930s by Ida Copeland and her husband and, together with 376 acres of park and woodland on the banks of the River Fal, given to the National Trust in 1955.

View over the River Fal from Trelissick Garden

Cornish gardens are noted for being spectacular in the spring and the best time to visit Trelissick is during late April and early May. But the planting here is more diversified than is usual in Cornwall, giving pleasure to the eye throughout the year. In summer there are late flowering shrubs, roses, lilies and mixed herbaceous borders edging beautiful lawns, and in September the different species of hydrangeas bloom. Trelissick stands on a bend in the River Fal, so deep here that there are usually several large container ships or cross-Channel ferries lying at anchor in its deep green waters, awaiting a decision on their futures. As you tour the garden the prospect over the river constantly changes, each a picture-postcard view that makes you reach for your camera.

Trelissick House is not open to the public, but at the entrance there is a National Trust shop with a good selection of books and a nursery selling plants propagated in the gardens. There is also a good restaurant in a converted Victorian barn serving traditional English fare: lamb and rosemary pipkin, spinach and almond flan, and salads. Last orders for lunch 2.15pm.

> The **Cornwall Crafts Association** has three galleries in Cornwall: Trelissick, Trelowarren (see Day Four) and Pencarrow (see Day Six). These excellent galleries display works by some of the most talented local artists and craftsmen. As well as examples of furniture, original paintings and patchwork quilts, there is a wide range of pottery, handknitted jumpers, jewellery, wooden objects and toys for sale in all price ranges.

Trelissick Garden, on the B3289 north of Feock. Tel: 0872 865808. King Harry Ferry takes cars across the River Fal from the foot of Trelissick Garden to the Roseland peninsula. It runs every 30 minutes all year, except Sun in winter
Opening times: Mar 1-Nov 1, Mon-Sat 10.30am-5.30pm; Sun 1-5.30pm
Admission: adult £3; child £1.50; NT members free

☆ TREWITHEN

Although Trewithen is most famous for its Cornish garden, it is worth timing your visit to coincide with the limited opening hours of the house itself. A simple, elegant Georgian mansion, built in the 1720s for comfort rather than show, it reflects the taste of a family which has always been discreet with its wealth, despite owning some of Cornwall's most profitable mines, china clay pits, and vast tracks of land. For the Hawkins family and their descendants, the Johnstones and now the Galsworthys, Trewithen has always been a main residence so it is surprising to discover that the interior and its contents have been little altered over the centuries.

The guided tour takes about an hour and includes the main ground-floor rooms. There is a glorious sitting room painted in a dusky yellow, as it was when Anne Hawkins redecorated in the 1760s, and a Rococo dining room, lined with fine family portraits (there are a number by Sir Joshua Reynolds at Trewithen) which have been fixed to the brick wall beneath the green-and-white plasterwork. Lovers of antique furniture will find much of interest including Chippendale chairs with their original tapestry seats and a Thomas Hancock spindle. There is nothing heavy-handed or over-the-top at Trewithen: the decor, the furniture, and the ornaments illustrate the refined elegance of the late 18th century.

The landscaped park was laid out in 1775 by Philip Hawkins but the highlight of Trewithen is its beautiful 30-acre garden, regarded as one of the finest in Cornwall today. Unlike the great Fox gardens (see Day Four) it has never suffered from periods of neglect so that the arrangement of the exotic trees and shrubs, designed to provide interest and colour on all levels, has been maintained. Before you tour the garden, it is worth viewing the 30-minute film on the garden's history, shown in the plant centre on the hour 11am-4pm.

The garden was created by George Johnstone in the 1920s, and his magnificent 200-yard-long serpentine lawn, stretching from the south front of the house and flanked by a kaleidoscope of colour, has greatly influenced modern garden design. Throughout the garden many of the exotic plants were raised from seeds collected in the wild, as well as cuttings from neighbouring gardens such as Caerhays. There are camellias, rhododendrons and magnolias in abundance, both Asian introductions and new species bred here, as well as rare Asiatic birches and maples. Unusually for Cornwall, Trewithen's garden is on fairly level ground, but what it lacks in countryside prospects is more than made up for by its succession of painterly scenes, the planting designed to offer fresh surprises at every turn in the path. The best time to visit is from mid-March until the end of May.

Trewithen's **nursery and plant centre** is considered to be the finest in Cornwall, with over 1,500 varieties on sale. Many have been hybridised and propagated here and this is the best place to come for rhododendrons, camellias, magnolias, clematis, azaleas and hydrangeas. The quality of the specimens is excellent and prices are very reasonable. The garden centre is open all year, Monday to Saturday, from 10am-5pm.

Trewithen, Probus (entrance on the A390 Truro-St Austell road). Tel: 0726 882764
Opening times: house - Mon and Tues Apr 1-Jul 31 and Aug Bank Hol 2-4.30pm; garden - Mon-Sat Mar 1-Sept 30, 10am-4.30pm
Admission: house - £2.80; garden - adult £2; child £1

TRURO

Cornwall's cathedral city and county capital is a pleasant place in which to spend the best part of a day, especially if the weather turns sour. Many of the 18th-century town houses and terraces remain intact and Lemon Street is considered the finest Georgian street west of Bath, although today doctors, dentists and solicitors occupy the rooms behind the golden stone façades. To appreciate the highlights of this elegant little city it is worth buying a copy of Bob Acton's *Landfall Book of Truro*, available locally, and following his descriptive city centre walk around the main sights.

The neat silhouette of **Truro Cathedral**, the first cathedral to be built in England for 700 years, soars above the city's skyline. (There is an impressive panoramic view over the city from Strangeways Terrace, to the left at the top of Lemon Street.) The Cathedral was built of granite in the Gothic style between 1880 and 1910 and in his *Buildings of England* Pevsner describes its interior as 'in many ways a *beau idéal* of the Early English style'. It contains no great monuments or exceptional sculpture, but its graceful vaulted nave is an impressive sight and the craftsmanship throughout is of the highest quality.

For those with an interest in architecture, Truro's new **Law Courts** certainly repay a visit. Designed by the firm of Evans and Shalev, this imaginative modern building has won several prestigious international awards. The combination of curved lines, grey and white colour scheme, and tall opaque windows successfully creates a sense of peace and well-being that must have a calming effect on those waiting to go into court. As a courtesy, check in at the reception desk before entering the main lobby.

The **Royal Cornwall Museum** contains something of everything: Egyptian mummies, doll's houses, model ships and finds from archaeological digs all over the county. It is probably of more interest to local schoolchildren doing projects than to the casual visitor. However, it does contain one of Britain's most important mineral collections, including part of the famous Menabilly Collection put together by Philip Rashleigh at the end of the 18th century and including specimens from as far afield as Russia. There is also an art gallery containing paintings by Cornwall's most famous artist, John Opie. A new wing, in a converted Methodist Chapel, displays changing exhibitions of modern art.

Truro Cathedral's West Front

The museum shop also contains the Arts Centre Trust box office which sells tickets for arts performances in and around Truro including the Three Spires Festival held in late June.

The Royal Cornwall County Museum and Art Gallery, River Street
Opening times: daily 9am-5pm, except Sun and Bank Hols
Admission: adult 75p; children free

Truro is the only place in Cornwall with good all-round shopping, ranging from big chain stores such as Marks and Spencer to charity shops selling all kinds of second-hand and ethnic goods. There are large indoor general markets in Lemon Street and on Lemon Quay, smart clothes shops, and there always seems to be an antiques fair taking place somewhere in town. In Old Bridge Street, The Guild of Ten sells the work of local craftsmen and is a good place to buy quality souvenirs. The **Tourist Information Centre** for Truro and the Roseland peninsula is located in the old City Hall in Boscawen Street; tel: 0872 74555.

From Easter to the end of October there are regular **boat trips** from the Town Quay to Falmouth taking in the main sights along the River Fal on the way. The round trip takes two hours, but you can return on a later boat. At low tide the boats cannot reach Truro so coaches take passengers down to Malpas to pick up the boat.

WHERE TO STAY

Falmouth
⌂ ✕ 🖃 **£££** ⍓

Penmere Manor Hotel, *Mongleath Road, Falmouth TR11 4PN*
Tel: 0326 211411
Open all year
Set in five acres of landscaped gardens just south of Falmouth this is a particularly comfortable family-run hotel. You can stay either in the Georgian main house or in the new garden wing where the rooms are more luxurious and spacious. Indoor facilities include a leisure club with an indoor pool, Jacuzzi, sauna and gym, and a games room; outside there is a heated pool, croquet lawn and a children's playground.
Bolitho's Restaurant offers both table d'hôte and à la carte dinner menus, based on fresh local produce.

St Agnes
⌂ ✕ 🐎 🖃 **£££** ⍓

Trevaunance Point Hotel,
Trevaunance Cove, St Agnes TR5 0RZ
Tel: 0872 553235
Open all year
Perched on the cliffside above the beach, this small ivy-clad hotel was

once a store for fishing gear with hammocks above for the weary. Now it has been converted into a comfortable eight-room hotel set in a tiny cliffside garden. All the bedrooms have sea views and are decorated in a tasteful cottagey style to complement the beamed ceilings and antique pieces. Downstairs, the bar and restaurant occupy another long low-beamed room. Local seafood is a speciality and there's a special vegetarian menu. The wine list includes offerings from all over the world, including China, Lebanon and Argentina. Last orders: lunch 2pm; dinner 9pm.

St Mawes
⌂ ✕ ⼍ ▭ **££** ⽒10

The Rising Sun, *St Mawes TR2 5DJ*
Tel: 0326 270233
Open all year
This sunny harbourside inn, owned by St Austell Brewery, has a lovely conservatory bar overlooking the water. Some bedrooms are on the small side, but all are well-equipped and decorated in a tasteful simple style. The restaurant, which serves English, French and Italian dishes, has a good reputation for its cooking. Last orders for dinner 9pm.

Veryan
⼍ ⼍ ✕ **£** ⽒14

Broom Parc, *Camels, Veryan TR2 5PJ*
Tel: 0872 501803
Open all year
This turn-of-the-century house, which featured in the television

adaptation of *The Camomile Law*n, stands alone in a magnificent cliff-top position on an exceptionally unspoilt part of the coast. There are three large double bedrooms, all with en suite shower rooms. Those at the front look straight out over the sea and seagulls fly past at window level. Guests share Keith and Lindsay Righton's lovely sitting room and good home cooking is served on request with vegetables from the garden. The pretty fishing hamlet of Portloe is a 20-minute walk away along the coastal footpath.

Veryan
⌂ ✕ ⼍ ▭ **££££** ⽒

The Nare Hotel, *Carne Beach, Veryan TR2 5PF*
Tel: 0872 501279
Open all year
This low white country house-style hotel stands on its own above a lovely sandy beach in Gerrans Bay. It is a bright, airy place with comfortable soft furnishings in pastel shades and floor-to-ceiling sliding doors making the most of the coastal views. Bedrooms are elegantly furnished with real and reproduction antiques; some have balconies or patios. The gardens contain a 50ft heated pool, a separate children's pool, and a tennis court. The table d'hôte dinner menu is fairly conservative but includes local seafood specialities and vegetarian dishes; the informal Gwendra Room serves light lunches. Last orders: lunch 2pm; dinner 9.30pm.

WHERE TO EAT

Carn Brea

✕ 🍽 ££ ⚹

Carn Brea Castle, *near Redruth (access from Carnkie near Four Lanes)*
Tel: 0209 218358
Closed Sun eve & Mon

Perched on the top of a tor, 750ft above sea-level, this restaurant occupies what was a hunting lodge. It is a wonderfully atmospheric place with walls of granite boulders and open log fires. The first-floor dining room seats around 20 and most tables have bird's eye views over the surrounding countryside. The menu concentrates on steaks and seafood, but also includes some Middle Eastern dishes (the owners are Jordanian) such as houmous with pitta bread and spicy sauces. Reserve ahead, especially for dinner and out of season. Last orders: lunch 2pm; dinner 9.30pm.

Malpas

🍽 🐴 ✕ £ ⚹

The Heron Inn, *Malpas, 2 miles south of Truro*
Tel: 0872 72773
Open all year
Situated at the confluence of the Fal, Truro and Tresillian rivers, this waterside inn is a lovely place for lunch or dinner, especially in summer when you can sit out on the terrace and admire the view. Simple, tasty fare: marinated chicken wings, liver and bacon kebab, ham and prawn mornay and steak casserole are menu regulars, served with chips or jacket potato. Parking is limited so arrive early in high season. Last orders: lunch 2pm; dinner 9.30pm.

Mithian

🍽 🐴 ✕ £ ⚹

The Miners Arms, *Mithian, near St Agnes*
Tel: 0872 552375
Open all year

This lovely 17th-century inn contains a warren of rooms full of character with low beams, and murals of Queen Elizabeth I and Blue Boy, painted at the turn of this century by a Dutchman in return for free drinks. The food is excellent, all home-made using fresh local produce, and includes crab bake, smoked haddock and white fish on spinach, barbecued ribs and curries. Children are welcome in the eating areas of the bar and there are trestle tables in the courtyard at the front. Last orders: lunch 2pm; dinner 9.30pm, later on busy summer days.

Mylor Bridge
🍴 🐴 ✉ £ 🕴

The Pandora Inn, *Restronguet Passage, Mylor Bridge, south of Falmouth*
Tel: 0326 72678
Open all year
This charming thatched pub on the banks of Restronguet creek is a rambling place filled with nautical paraphernalia. You can order from the bar or be served in the restaurant, and in fine weather there is plenty of seating outside on a floating pontoon. The menu is strong on fish and seafood, the dish of the day depending on the local catch. It can become very crowded in summer when parking is difficult. Summer last orders: lunch 2.30pm; dinner 10pm.

Truro
✗ ▬ ££ 🕴

Bustopher Jones, *62 Lemon Street, Truro*
Tel: 0872 79029
Closed Sun lunch
This stylish panelled wine bar, arranged on several different levels, serves some of the best food in Truro, all home-made and including dishes from all over the world. You can start with guacamole, crab pâté, or burritos, and move on to jambalaya, liver and bacon hot pot or fish of the day. A number of good wines are served by the glass. It is popular with local professionals and is a very pleasant place for lunch or dinner. Last orders: lunch 2pm; dinner 10pm.

THE HELFORD
RIVER AND
THE LIZARD

Curiously the Lizard peninsula is by-passed by many holiday-makers who head straight for St Ives and Land's End, or else visit Lizard Point, the most southerly place in Britain, and whip straight out again. This lack of heavy holiday traffic makes the Lizard an appealing place for those in search of the simple plea-sures of life. Within a labyrinth of sinuous minor roads trapped between high Cornish hedges you will discover fine Jacobean manors, timeless rural hamlets, and sandy coves and creeks unspoilt by modern development.

The landscape constantly changes and if you follow the Lizard Drive, described on page 73, you will appreciate the quiet beauty of this area: the magnificent cliffscapes of the wild west coast, the wind-swept heathlands and, on its almost sultry eastern shores, sheltered valleys whose micro-climates favour lush sub-tropical plants. Further north, the Helford River and its tidal creeks over-hung with sessile oaks can be explored on foot or by boat. On the north side of the river are several important Cornish gardens: Trebah, Glendurgan and Penjerrick.

Children will enjoy the Seal Sanctuary at Gweek, beaches perfect for building sandcastles and learning to swim, and Flambards theme park. If the weather is wet you can tour Goonhilly, Britain's largest satellite telecommunications station, whose large dish aerials are visible from miles around, or hole up in one of the area's excellent pubs.

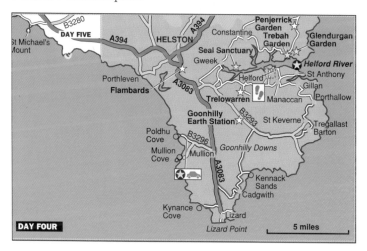

☆ FLAMBARDS

Anyone hoping for a Cornish version of Alton Towers or Chessington will find Flambards triple theme park a disappointment. Of course, it doesn't pretend to be a high-tech pleasure park but the admission cost is fairly steep for a family, and you may not think it good value. It is a popular choice in wet weather but although much is under cover, the things that children will enjoy most - the rides and the Aero Park - are open to the elements and present a somewhat depressing prospect in the rain.

The park's highlight is the under-cover Victorian village, an authentic reconstruction of more than 50 shops, trade premises and interiors. The attention to period detail is superb, and life-size waxworks help to recreate typical Victorian scenes, from the livery stables to the pipe yard wash-house. There are thousands of everyday artefacts, from a window display of corsets and stays to the complete range of goods that could be found in a general store, all kept in pristine condition. The one drawback is the lack of explanation; a detailed guide would enhance the value of the collection. A particularly interesting exhibit is the chemist's shop which came lock, stock and barrel from South Petherton in Somerset where it had been sealed off after the apothecary's death in 1909.

Flambards Victorian Village

From the Victorian village, visitors move to Britain in the Blitz where a full-scale street and interiors recreate day-to-day life during the Second World War, from the interior of an Anderson shelter to a typical dress shop window. As you walk around you hear the whine of air-raid warnings, the falling of bombs and the calming words of Winston Churchill. A Battle of Britain war gallery displays photographs and artefacts of the forces in action, and there is an impressive display of some of the most dramatic photographs taken during the London Blitz.

The outdoor Aero Park contains 24 aircraft, both vintage and modern, and visitors are allowed to climb into the cockpits of a number of them. The rest of the complex is a combination of adventure playground and superior fairground rides: water chutes, giant slides, a tame roller coaster, merry-go-round and aerial rides. These can become very crowded in high summer, and will probably appeal most to children under 10. There are various indifferent food outlets and souvenir shops, a shooting gallery and the inevitable computer games, which will mean digging into your pocket again.

Flambards, off the B3083 just south of Helston. Tel: 0326 564093
Opening times: daily Easter–Oct 31, 10am–5.30pm (last admission 4pm); during Aug
the park closes at 8pm (last admission 5.30pm)
Admission: adult £7.50; child 4-14 £6.50

☆ GLENDURGAN GARDEN

This classic Cornish valley garden is one of a trio created by the
Fox family in the mid-19th century (the others are Penjerrick and
Trebah) which are open to the public. The Foxes were Quakers,
grown prosperous on shipping and fishing interests in
Falmouth, and as keen gardeners they wanted to demonstrate
'the great miracle of Nature' by bringing together species from
all over the world. At Glendurgan there is a 'Holy Bank' with the
Tree of Heaven, the Judas Tree and the Crown of Thorns. Unlike
the other Fox gardens which have suffered long periods of
neglect this century, Glendurgan has always been well kept up
by the family and has belonged to the National Trust since 1962.

The 25-acre garden spreads over four shallow valleys that lead
down eventually to the former fishing hamlet of Durgan, now
turned into holiday cottages, and a beach of dark sand strewn
with large boulders which visitors can use. It is at its best in
spring, from late March until the end of May, and has century-
old camellias and rhododendrons. In the woodland areas, Lent
lilies, bluebells and columbines thrive as do bamboos, tree ferns
and hydrangeas (September flowering) in the moist lower valley.
The cherry laurel maze, planted by Alfred Fox in 1833, is a highlight of the garden, although it is currently undergoing restoration and visitors are not allowed to enter it for the time being.

Glendurgan Garden, 1 mile south of Mawnan Smith. Tel: 0326 250906
Opening times: Mar 1–end Oct, Tues–Sat and Bank Hol Mons, 10.30am–5.30pm
Admission: adult £2.50; child £1.25; NT members free

☆ GOONHILLY EARTH STATION

In the midst of the Goonhilly Downs National Nature Reserve is
the incongruous sight of ten dish aerials with spans of up to
100ft silently communicating with satellites in space. This is the
world's largest satellite earth station, transmitting television pro-

grammes all over the world, receiving foreign correspondents' film reports for the national news, and dealing with tens of millions of international telephone calls each year. Things have come a long way since 1901 when, just a few miles away in Poldhu, Marconi sent the first transatlantic 'wire-less' signal.

British Telecom has built a visitors' centre at the station where you can find out all about these silent communicators and it is a popular place on cloudy summer days. There is a 35-minute guided tour of the site by bus during which you learn the history and function of each of the dishes and visit the operations control centre where banks of television screens monitor programmes being relayed and received.

Goonhilly Earth Station

Inside the centre you can view an interesting nature documentary on Goonhilly Downs, showing grass snakes, adders and lizards basking beneath the dishes, and learn about the rare Cornish heath that surrounds the station. There is a small museum of communications artefacts and several hands-on exhibits where you can watch your speech pattern being reproduced electronically and find out how telephone exchanges work. The licensed cafeteria is an appealing place for lunch, serving pasties, flans, salads and daily specials which are well prepared and good value.

Before you leave here take a stroll out of the gates and along one of the heathland nature trails. Don't worry about the adders, they are fortunately shy and retiring creatures. In summer the wild flowers put on a magnificent display, attracting many species of butterflies, and in September the flowering heather turns the whole area a beautiful pinky-purple, broken only by splashes of yellow gorse. A large variety of birds breed on the heath: curlews, lapwings, skylarks and yellowhammers among them, and buzzards and falcons hover in search of voles and fieldmice.

Goonhilly Earth Station, on the B3293 3 miles west of St Keverne. Tel: 0326 22333
Opening times: daily Easter-Oct 10am-6pm
Admission: adult £3; child 5-15, £1.50

THE HELFORD RIVER

The Helford River is one of the most beautiful places in Cornwall. A drowned valley known in geographical terms as a ria, it formed an effective natural barrier isolating the Lizard from the rest of the Cornwall until the arrival of motorised transport. Even today there is a real sense of remoteness here, especially west of Helford village where the tidal creeks cut deep into hills covered in ancient oak woodland. It has also remained unspoilt by modern intrusions, thanks to the restraint of local landowners, like the Vyvyans of Trelowarren, who refused to sell land to developers.

Small quays served the estates, and through the ages the Helford was a popular haunt of smugglers. In 1602 chronicler Richard Carew wrote that it was nicknamed Stealford and attracted 'only the worst sort of seafarers... whose guilty breasts, with an eye in their backs, look warily how they may go out ere they will adventure to enter'. Frenchman's Creek, the inspiration for Daphne du Maurier's novel of the same name, may have been named after the activities of a French pirate ship according to local historians. The best way to explore these tidal creeks is on foot or by boat. On the south side there are car parks only at St Anthony-in-Meneage and Helford village.

Boat excursions along the Helford River leave from Falmouth and St Mawes (see Day Three), but at St Anthony-in-Meneage you can hire self-drive motorboats, Wayfarer and Drascombe sail-boats from Anthony Jenkin (reserve ahead by telephoning 0326 23357). A half-day's hire costs around £30 and it takes an hour to reach Frenchman's Creek from St Anthony.

Helford village is enchanting: thatched cottages climb away from its narrow creek where swans and ducks swim; there is a tea garden, an excellent waterside pub, The Shipwright's Arms (see Where to Eat), and the general store selling Roskilly Farm ice-cream. Beyond the pub a path leads through to the main river where you can catch a small ferry across to Helford Passage, a 20-minute walk away from Trebah and Glendurgan gardens.

FRENCHMAN'S CREEK WALK

This hour-long circular walk takes in one of the most beautiful stretches of the Helford River, particularly breathtaking in the early morning sun. From Helford village car park walk down the hill but do not cross the bridge. Instead take the footpath signposted Manaccan which winds through woodland carpeted in wild flowers. Where the path divides, take the right fork and carry on through the middle of Kestle Farm and pick up the path signposted Frenchman's Pill ('pill' is Cornish for creek) to the water's edge.

Helford River from Frenchman's Creek

At low tide the creek is reduced to a trickle of water snaking through mud, so try to time your walk nearer high tide. Even on a sunny day the creek has an eerie, haunted feel; the twisted branches of the ancient sessile oaks lean far out over the water as if reaching for something hidden in its depths. Dead branches rise from the grey-green water, the trees cast giant shadows, and only the cool air betrays that this is not a tropical swamp. It is almost a relief to climb on to open ground again.

From the top of the hill there are fabulous views up the Helford River and across to Groyne Point, whose woodlands have been coppiced over the centuries but never cut down. After climbing a stile, turn right on to the lane where a fine view downstream unfolds as you round a bend. Immediately after the cattle grid turn left down a track signposted Pengwedhen between splendid examples of Cornish hedges. Take the right-hand fork to Penarvon Cove, picking your way across the muddy beach to reach the tarmac lane that leads into Helford, emerging at the Shipwright's Arms.

✪ LIZARD DRIVE

This drive covers some of the small gems which make the Lizard such a rewarding place to visit. It will take around four hours, longer if you stroll along the beaches and the nature trails. From the main A3083 Helston-Lizard road turn right to **Mullion**, the largest settlement on the peninsula but still no more than a village. If the wind is blowing, visit Cornish Kites which has a large selection of kites of both simple and elaborate design. The loveliest of the beaches here is **Poldhu Cove**, signposted in the village, an unspoilt stretch of sand backed by dunes and protected by cliffs on both sides with a typical beach café and a lifeguard in summer.

From Mullion return to the main road and just before Lizard turn right to **Kynance Cove**. This masterpiece of coastal erosion has attracted tourists since the 18th century. From the cliff-top car park it is a 10-minute walk down to the beach, best visited at low tide, when a large expanse of sand is revealed and the 200ft-cliffs create a perfect sun trap. You can walk around the 'islands', great stacks of rare serpentine - a lustrous black rock mottled and veined with red, green and white - that give the place such character. There are also some impressive caves to explore.

Turn right when you reach the main road again to visit the village of **Lizard** where local craftsmen cut and polish serpentine. Hardy's sells the best quality souvenirs: all kinds of boxes, bowls, lamp bases and frames. Red serpentine is rare and commands the highest prices. Lizard Point, the most southerly place on mainland Britain, is not of great interest, so return along the A3083 and take the first right to Cadgwith.

Cadgwith is the prettiest fishing village on the Lizard, a collection of white-washed stone cottages, many still thatched, around a tiny beach. Fishermen still go out for lobster and crab and winch their boats up on to the beach. Park in the official car park and walk down. The Old Cellars is open all day (April to November) for light meals, cream teas and delicious fresh crab sandwiches. From June to September, the Crows Nest gallery sells local crafts and watercolours by talented local artists (which is not usually the case) at reasonable prices.

Cadgwith

If you want to find a safe place for a swim, head out of Cadgwith through Ruan Minor and Kuggar, where cottage gardens are filled with exotic plants, to **Kennack Sands**. Although there are several caravan sites above the beach making it very crowded in high summer, this is where generations of locals and holiday-makers have come to learn to swim. Back in Kuggar turn right after the pub and head over Goonhilly Downs. Where the heathland road meets the B3293, turn right for Coverack. After you pass the left turn for St Keverne you reach a crossroads. Go straight ahead down the unmarked road (called Main Dale on the Ordnance Survey map) across a beautiful heathland to Tregallast Barton.

Tregallast Barton is an interesting organic dairy farm and the home of **Roskilly ice-cream**, the finest in Cornwall. The flavours on sale depend on what's been made recently in the dairy next door and may include tiramisu and hazelnut meringue, banana custard, and Hokey Pokey, a delicious soft honeycomb mixture. There are also home-made jams, chutneys, mustards, and clotted cream for sale. Take your cornet and go for a walk along the farm's nature trail. This 20-acre conservation area includes ponds, traditional meadows and old orchards as well as fine examples of Cornish hedges where native shrubs and trees are set in stock-proof barriers of stone and soil. In the late afternoon you can also see the cows being milked from a viewing gallery, and children can visit and feed the calves during the day. The shop and the nature trail are open every day all year, until dusk in summer. The ice-cream counter itself is closed from mid-November until April.

From Tregallast Barton pass through St Keverne, still very much a locals' village, and head for Porthallow and the **Five Pilchards Inn**. The interior of this unspoilt pub, frequented by local fishermen, is something of a seafaring museum. Around its walls are photographs and newspaper reports of ships wrecked on the notorious Manacles offshore, and from the ceiling hang all sorts of nautical paraphernalia. Excellent lobster and crab salads are served from noon-2pm, as well as pasties and ploughman's lunches (no children's room). From here it is an easy drive along rural lanes to the banks of the Helford River.

☆ PENJERRICK GARDEN

Early this century Penjerrick was considered to be the finest garden in Cornwall, imaginatively planted with an extraordinary variety of semi-tropical trees and shrubs from all over the world, some of which would grow and flower nowhere else in Britain. Sadly this Fox family garden became neglected after the First World War, reverting to an overgrown wilderness until the 1980s. There is now one gardener, Jane Bird, who with volunteer help is trying to restore the garden to something of its past glory.

If you are knowledgeable about plants, you will be astonished at the number of rare exotics growing so healthily here. If not, you may find this overgrown woodland garden less visually appealing than Trelissick (see Day Three) and Trebah although it is

spectacular in April and May when the rhododendrons and azaleas flower. Because Penjerrick is less visited than other Cornish
gardens you can find peace and tranquillity within its 29 acres
even in high summer. Narrow paths meander down through an
undulating valley, taking you into jungles of bamboo, laurel and
fern before opening out to reveal fine prospects down the valley
to the sea.

Jane Bird is happy to take interested gardeners on a guided tour
pointing out the stars of the collection, as few are labelled, but
telephone ahead. The Edinburgh Royal Botanic Garden has
recently chosen Penjerrick as the site for its new collection of
endangered temperate trees and associated plants from South
America, California and New Zealand and Mexico, continuing
the garden's tradition as a kind of plantsman's theme park.

Penjerrick Garden, on the Mawman Smith-Budock Water road. Tel: 0326 250074
Opening times: Mar-Sept, Wednes and Sun 1.30-4.30pm; by prior arrangement at
other times
Admission: adult £1.50; child 75p

☆ ## SEAL SANCTUARY

At Gweek, the highest navigable point on the Helford River, the
Cornish Seal Sanctuary and Marine Animal Rescue Centre
stands in 45 acres of landscaped grounds beside the river. The
sanctuary takes in grey Atlantic seal pups who have lost their
mothers in storms, returning them to the sea once they can catch
their own fish suppers. Some of the more seriously injured seals
become permanent residents and take part in the breeding pro-
gramme. It is an interesting, informative place to visit, designed
to create greater environmental awareness.

In the reception centre there are good educational displays on
the lives of marine mammals and the ways in which we are pol-
luting our seas and rivers. Tanks contain examples of river fish
under threat. A 12-minute video discusses the lives of seals, how
they became an endangered species, and the role of the sanctuary. Downstairs is a tropical aquarium with clown fish, sea
anemones, carp and tetras among its many brightly coloured
inhabitants.

From here visitors can walk or take an open bus (wheelchairs
can be rolled on) to the seal hospital. It usually contains some

rather sad-looking baby seals, who despite being ill have to put up with the constant tramp of visitors and the noise of another video designed to persuade you to part with more money. The path continues down to fenced-in pools alongside the river where you can watch young and old seals in what appear to be frantic swimming races, or simply snoozing on the grass, idly flapping their flippers. If you want to see real action, visit the pools at 11am or 4pm (3.30pm in winter) when the seals are fed. Yellow-crested Macaroni penguins are also bred here.

Seals at play in the pool at Gweek's Seal Sanctuary

The sanctuary occupies another beautiful stretch of the Helford River and through telescopes you can get a close look at curlews, shell ducks and herons hunting for fish in the narrow channel that meanders through the mudbanks at low tide. There's a woodland walk which takes you alongside the creek for more delightful views down river and a pleasant café selling soft drinks, cakes and light snacks. In summer burgers and hot dogs are grilled on an open-air barbecue.

Cornish Seal Sanctuary, on the north bank of the Helford at Gweek. Tel: 032 622 361
Opening times: daily all year (except Christmas Day) 9.30am-6pm
Admission: adult £4; children over 4, £2; reduced rates in winter

☆ TREBAH GARDEN

When Major Hibbert and his wife Eira acquired Trebah in November 1981 they thought they had bought a pleasant 18th-century house in 26 acres of self-maintaining woodland and looked forward to a retired life of leisure. 'After we'd been here a week a chap came and introduced himself as secretary of the Cornwall Gardens Society, then asked me how many gardeners we were going to employ,' says Major Hibbert. 'He said the garden had been neglected for 50 years and, if it went on any longer, it would reach the point of no return. Of course, he lied through his teeth - it had already gone past the point of no return.'

The Hibberts bravely took up the challenge and have achieved a miracle of restoration, returning this mature 19th-century Fox garden to the prominence it enjoyed early this century. It is predominantly a spring flowering garden, containing more than 1,500 specimens of trees and shrubs from all over the world, but there is interest here all year. It is perhaps the most dramatically situated of Cornwall's show gardens, the weird and wonderful trees and shrubs clinging to the sides of a steep ravine above a stream which feeds ponds as it tumbles down to the Helford River.

The sheer size of its exotic trees is impressive, from the magnificent Monterey pines to the three stately Chusan palms, the tallest in Britain. The rhododendrons have grown as tall as trees here and, in April and May, their flowers unfold in a fabulous spectrum of pinks, reds and mauves recreating a Himalayan landscape. To walk through Gunnera Passage is to feel Lilliputian as the sandpaper leaves of this Brazilian rhubarb close over your head. At the bottom a gate leads out to a private beach where visitors are welcome to sunbathe, swim and eat picnics.

A real effort has been made to encourage children to take an interest in the garden. They have their own special guide, *Tracking the Trebah Trail*, a treasure hunt in search of hidden wooden shapes which also reveals the garden's special trees and shrubs. There's also a play area with climbing frame, ropes and hammocks beneath a giant cedar tree.

Trebah Garden, on the Mawnan Smith-Helford Passage road. Tel: 0326 250448
Opening times: daily all year, 10.30am-5pm
Admission: adult £2.50; child 5-15 £1

Exotic Trebah Garden

The village stores and Post Office in Constantine near Trebah Garden holds a few surprises. Inside is one of the largest off-licences in the west of England with 200 different kinds of malt whisky, vintage ports, wines, Champagnes, Cognacs, and a large selection of the more exotic alcoholic drinks from around the world. **Constantine Stores** at 30 Fore Street is open Monday-Saturday 9am-1pm, 2-5.30pm and 10am-noon on Sunday. Tel: 0326 40226.

☆ TRELOWARREN

This is not one of Cornwall's great manor houses, but the estate is an ancient one, predating the Norman Conquest, and covers 1,000 acres stretching down to the Helford River. Since the 15th century it has been the family seat of the Vyvyans, although part is now leased to the Christian Fellowship which operates it as a retreat. You can join a guided tour but there is little of interest to see. The Elizabethan house was remodelled in Victorian times and, apart from a few portraits, none of the family furnishings remain. The highlight is the chapel's interior, decorated in the neo-Gothic Strawberry Hill style fashionable in the 1820s and accessible without touring the house. It has excellent acoustics and concerts are often held here on Sundays in summer.

The Georgian stable block alongside the house has been convert-ed into a gallery, workshops and a restaurant. Here you will find another of the Cornwall Crafts Association's excellent galleries displaying some of the finest Cornish workmanship in furniture, woodcarving and design. Next door is Trelowarren Pottery where Nic Harrison hand-throws mugs, jugs, casseroles and dis-tinctive bread bins, while his wife Jackie Harrison weaves rag rugs on a loom. The Bistro Restaurant is open for lunch and din-ner (see Where to Eat).

Trelowarren's estate walk covers 6 miles of woodland paths, marked with blobs of paint, although the route is unclear in places. It is a lovely peaceful place to stroll on a warm summer's day and you will find yourself alone along much of the route, although there is a campsite on the eastern fringe of the estate. Definitely worth seeking out is the ancient Celtic Halligye Fogou, a man-made cave which is 90ft long and 6ft high, used either for defence or as part of sun worship rituals. It is found about 700 yards west of the house near two thatched cottages and is marked on the Ordnance Survey map.

Trelowarren House, signposted on the B3293 after Garras. Tel: 0326 22366
Opening times: House open Easter-end Sept, Wednes and Bank Hol Mons 2.30-5pm;
woodland walk open dawn-dusk Apr-Sept; Gallery open daily except Mon end Mar-
mid-Dec; Pottery open 11am-5pm weekdays all year

Trelowarren House

WHERE TO STAY

Constantine
⌂ ✕ ⚥ ▭ ££ ⚣

Trengilly Wartha, *Nancenoy,*
Constantine, Falmouth TR11 5RP
Tel: 0326 40332
Open all year
This family-run country inn stands in its own peaceful grounds above the Helford River. The recently renovated bedrooms are bright and fresh-looking and half have large en suite bathrooms. Downstairs there are two cosy bars (it is a freehouse), a games room and a family room as well as a more formal restaurant with an imaginative dinner menu based on fresh local produce such as crab and spring onion tartlets and lamb roasted with herbs and walnuts. Good bar meals are also available. Last orders: lunch 2pm; dinner 9.30pm.

Gillan
⌂ ✕ ⚥ ▭ ££ ⚣

Tregildry Hotel, *Gillan, Manaccan,*
Helston TR12 6HG
Tel: 0326 23378
Open beg Apr - mid-Oct
There are fabulous views over Gillan Creek and Falmouth Bay from this friendly 11-room hotel run by the Norton family which offers the best

value in the area. A footpath leads down to a shingle beach and there are lovely walks along the Helford River from here. Bedrooms are light, airy and prettily decorated, most with en suite bathrooms. The restaurant has a very good reputation for its imaginative cooking based on fresh local produce. Non-residents should reserve in advance.

Manaccan

🏠 🐴 ✉ £ ⅓3

Tregonwell Farm, *Manaccan, Helston TR12 6HS*
Tel: 0326 23457
Open all year
This plain-looking farmhouse on a dairy farm surprises guests with its inside comforts. Penny Williams has decorated her three bedrooms simply but with flair. All share one large bathroom, and downstairs there is a handsome dining room and a cosy sitting room for guests. Penny's breakfasts are legendary and include freshly squeezed orange juice. Good suppers can be found at New Inn in Manaccan, a 10-minute walk away.

Mullion

🏠 ✕ 🐴 ▭ ££££ ⅓

Polurrian Hotel, *Mullion, The Lizard TR12 7EN*
Tel: 0326 240421
Open beg Apr-end Dec
This is the finest hotel on the Lizard: a handsome white building in clifftop gardens above its own sandy bay. The 40 bedrooms are tastefully decorated in a smart country house style, many with expansive views over Mounts Bay. A recent addition is the leisure club containing a heated indoor pool, sauna, solarium and gym. Outside there is another heated pool, tennis court and a croquet lawn and towards sunset it is delightful to take a turn along the coastal path which runs in front of the hotel. Children are well catered for with their own activity room and play area in the garden, and baby listening service. The hotel's own fishing boat brings in some of the fish suppers, and vegetables and salads come from its own greenhouses. Non-residents should reserve ahead. Last orders: lunch 1.45pm; dinner 8.45pm.

WHERE TO EAT

Helford

✕ ▭ ££££ ⅓

The Riverside, *Helford, Helston*
Tel: 0326 23443
Open early Mar - mid-Nov; dinner only
Several village cottages have been converted into this cosy restaurant with rooms overlooking the creek. The cooking has a French bias, but the ingredients are local - fresh fish, lamb and game in season - and it is known for its unusual pâtés and soufflés. Expect to pay London prices. Good wine list. The bed-

rooms are prettily decorated but on the small side. Dinner served 7.30-9.30pm.

Helford

🍴 🐴 ✉ £ ⅓

The Shipwright's Arms, *Helford Village*
Tel: 0326 23235
Open 11am-11pm all year, except Sun afternoons
This lovely old inn, once a favourite haunt of smugglers, has a large waterside terrace where barbecue

dinners are cooked in summer. Otherwise, there is plenty of seating in the cosy beamed bars where the blackboard menu includes a good selection of home-made fare: soups, garlic mushrooms, beef in beer, jumbo prawns and lobster salad. Last orders: lunch 2pm; dinner 9pm.

Manaccan

ⅰ ⅰ ☗ ☒ £ ☖12

The New Inn, *Manaccan village*
Tel: 0326 23323
Open all year
This 17th-century inn has recently become a listed building and its snug bar is popular with locals, who often end up serving the drinks while the barman plays cards. Penny Williams, who offers B&B at Tregonwell Farm, is the cook here and very good the food is too. At lunchtimes there are home-made soups, pasties and American-style sandwiches, while in the evening the blackboard menu includes the catch of the day, chilli, pies and steaks. Cream teas are served in summer from 3-5.30pm. Last orders: lunch 2pm; dinner 9pm (later if busy).

Mawgan

☒ ☒ ££ ☖

The Yard Bistro, *Trelowarren, near Mawgan*
Tel: 0326 22595
Open Easter-Christmas; open Thurs-Sat only in winter
Located in a converted carriage house alongside Trelowarren House, this smart bistro comprises of a large bar and a dining room with an open fire. The menu concentrates on imaginative versions of classic dishes: cream of Stilton and fennel soup, hot avocado with crab and prawns, fillet of pork with stewed aubergines and

black olives, steamed red bream in a tomato and sherry vinaigrette. The Sunday lunch set menu offers particularly good value. Reserve ahead, especially in winter. Last orders: lunch 2pm; dinner 9pm.

Porthleven

ⅰ ⅰ ☗ ☒ £ ☖

The Ship Inn, *Porthleven*
Tel: 0326 572841
Open all year; 11.30 am-11 pm Jul and Aug
This characterful 17th-century inn is built into the rocks and is a real sun-trap on sunny winter days when you can sit outside and admire the harbour views. You can eat either in the bar or in a separate dining room. The menu is extensive but all the food appears to be home-made and fish is a speciality. Specials may include fish and meat pies, vegetable curry, and crab thermidor as well as huge seafood platters and excellent sandwiches. There is a family room. Last orders: lunch 2.30 pm, dinner 9.30 pm (no food served Sunday evening in winter).

THE LAND'S END
PENINSULA

The Land's End peninsula is Cornwall in microcosm. Wild headlands, sheltered sandy coves, characterful fishing villages, abandoned tin mines, exotic gardens and prehistoric settlements - all are to be found in this most westerly part of Britain. The ports of Penzance and St Ives, which have provided inspiration for generations of artists, are full of charm and interest. Land's End is on every visitor's itinerary and, despite the commercialism, a walk around its golden granite cliffs is not to be missed. Neither is the North Coast Drive from St Ives to St Just which passes through a timeless Celtic landscape.

The peninsula's other highlights include St Michael's Mount which rises so dramatically from Mounts Bay and the open-air Minack Theatre built into the cliffs near Porthcurno. Solitude is surprisingly easy to find. Even in August you can find yourself alone on the starkly beautiful moors that cover most of the peninsula, littered with the remains of prehistoric settlements like Chysauster, stone circles and ancient forts. The idyllic sandy beaches found along the south coast and around St Ives Bay provide safe swimming for children who will also enjoy visiting the parrots and exotic rainforest birds at Paradise Park.

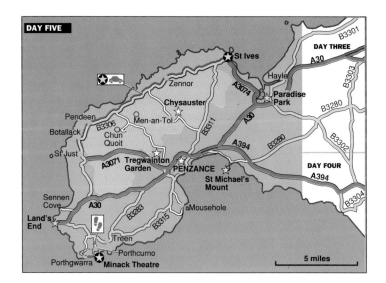

 ☆ # CHYSAUSTER

The remains of this ancient village are the best preserved in Cornwall as much archaeological work has been done here and, unlike similar settlements in the area, the stones have not been removed to build later dwellings. Its site, on the edge of moorland, is magnificent with panoramic views over Mounts Bay and a large swathe of countryside to the west. There are eight circular courtyard houses dating back to at least Roman times, including a semi-detached pair. Paved paths lead up to their entrances which face away from the westerlies that could knock you off your feet on this exposed site.

It is worth buying the guidebook which explains the functions of the different rooms. Each house also has a garden terrace, and a network of covered channels leading to rainwater collection pits. The walls are several feet thick and still reach almost their original height; only the thatched roofs are missing. To help you complete the picture of this ancient farming community there are mounted artists' impressions of scenes from village life. It all looks far more comfortable than one would have imagined.

Chysauster Ancient Village, turn off the B3311 Penzance-St Ives road at Badger's Cross and follow signs
Opening times: Good Fri or Apr 1-end Sept, daily 10am-6pm
Admission: adult £1.20; children over 6 90p

☆ LAND'S END

Land's End was famous as far back as Roman times, when it was known as Belerion - 'Seat of Storms'. Today visitors come here from all over the world but for many it proves an anti-climax. Its significance is lost when you arrive by car and simply look out over the cliff-top, but in the past it had a place in every sailor's heart. For those setting off on long ocean voyages, Land's End was their last sight of a homeland to which they might never return. To appreciate the beauty and romance of this most westerly tip of Britain, it is best to avoid the man-made attractions of the Land's End Experience altogether. Drive instead to Sennen Cove and walk from there.

There is a large car park on the left before you reach Sennen. From here turn left on to the lane which joins the cliff-top footpath to Dr Syntax's Head, the true land's end, a distance of just over a mile on the flat. If you have time, carry on past the First and Last House and around Land's End itself to Pordenack Point or Nanjizal, from where you can take inland footpaths across fields back to Sennen. Along this stretch is some of the finest scenery on Cornwall's coastal path, the granite rock turned golden by lichens. High cliffs have been weathered into sheer rock pillars, arches and giant stepped boulders around which the blue-green waters of the Atlantic froth and foam.

If you have children or the weather is poor, you may be tempted to visit the theme park. It was created by Peter de Savary who bought Land's End in 1987 (he has since sold it) and while he rescued it from scruffiness, the entertainment complex does destroy any sense of remoteness. The exhibitions are fairly educational and informative, but there is a sensationalism, especially on the subject of wrecking, that local people find objectionable. Man Against the Sea looks at some of the most famous shipwrecks off Land's End with a video showing the work of the Coastguard Service including dramatic footage of lifeboat rescues in stormy seas. You will also learn about the formation of the Land's End peninsula, early Celtic settlements, and the history of seafaring in the area through well presented audio-visual displays. Don't miss the beautiful collection of model ships, from the Endeavour to a traditional Cornish lugger, made by Ted George, a retired carpenter from nearby Penberth.

The complex's main attraction is a dramatic sound and light show, the Last Labyrinth, a mixture of fanciful tales of smugglers, pirates and wreckers in Cornwall and a confusingly condensed version of the legend of King Arthur. Of more interest is the account of the Fastnet yachting disaster, using rescue service commentary and dramatic photographs. Given the build-up the show is something of an anti-climax, and small children may be disturbed by the loud sound effects.

A small train takes visitors to the outdoor attractions: the First and Last House, now a souvenir shop; Greeb Cottage, a former croft where you can watch craftsmen at work, see Cornwall's landmarks in miniature and visit farm animals; and, of course, Land's End itself. There are also adventure playgrounds, gift shops, an art gallery and food outlets, including a pleasant conservatory bar in the State House Hotel.

Land's End, follow the A30 from Penzance. Tel: 0736 87150
Opening times: daily (except Christmas Day) 10am-5pm, later in mid-summer
Admission: adult £4.50; children under 16 free (but this may change)

> For a bird's eye view of the coast you can take a **pleasure flight** from Land's End aerodrome (turn right off A30 at Crows an Wra) in a 3-seater Cessna. The trips range from a quick 5-minute flip over Land's End and Sennen Cove costing £14 a person to a half-hour tour of the coast from Penzance to St Ives for £40. In summer you can simply turn up and hop on a 'plane any time between 9.30am and 5.30pm. For more information telephone 0736 788771.

✪ MINACK THEATRE

Few open-air theatres in the world can boast a more impressive backdrop than the Minack: a natural granite amphitheatre on the very edge of sheer cliffs which curve around an azure bay ending in a jagged promontory. The theatre is a memorial to an extraordinary woman, Rowena Cade, who transformed her cliffside garden into a magical theatre in the style of the ancient Greeks, doing much of the building work herself right up until her death in 1983.

Her love affair with the Minack began in 1932 when she provided a site for local village players to stage Shakespeare's *The*

Tempest. People were so moved by the beauty of the cliff at night, that regular annual performances were held. After the Second World War Miss Cade slowly expanded the theatre, building seating, balustrades and balcony boxes on tiny ledges. Dressed granite was too expensive so she used concrete, decorating it with lettering and intricate Celtic designs using the tip of a screwdriver.

In the exhibition centre at the entrance there is a slide show and commentary on the history of the theatre and a photographic display of its greatest successes. But the best way to appreciate this remarkable theatre is to attend a performance. In keeping with the original spirit, most of the productions are put on by amateur theatrical companies from all over Britain. They range from Shakespeare plays to musicals and adaptations of classic novels. The season lasts from the end of May to mid-September and half of the 800 seats are sold on the day of the performance. In peak season it's best to arrive around 6pm; the box office opens at 6.45pm. Parties of more than eight can reserve in advance.

The Minack Theatre, Porthcurno. Reservations tel: 0736 810471; other enquiries 0736 810694
Opening times: Easter-Oct 31, daily 10am-6pm except matinee days
Performances: matinees 1.30-2pm; evening 8pm
Admission: theatre viewing, adult £1.40; child 5-16 50p; show tickets, adult £4; child £2

Performance in the Minack Theatre

Around the headland from the Minack Theatre is **Porthcurno Beach**, one of the finest on the Land's End peninsula. There is a large car park and sandy tracks lead down to the funnel-shaped beach which is protected from the wind by tall granite cliffs on both sides. It is safe for bathing and has a lifeguard in season.

Porthcurno Beach

GRANITE COAST WALK

This 90-minute circular walk takes in a particularly beautiful stretch of the coastal path, a favourite local bathing beach and an interesting church. Park in the large car park in Porthgwarra and turn left on to the footpath to St Levan. The path is quite steep in places as it wends its way over granite outcrops and stray boulders. From the cliff-top there are magnificent views as far as Lizard Point. At the acorn sign, take the right fork along the cliffside path. The granite blocks below have been eroded into weird and wonderful shapes which you can imagine into sleeping dogs, sunbathing women or anything else that takes your fancy.

Further along is the remote sandy cove of Porthchapel, a great place for sunbathing and swimming at low tide. A short flight of steps leads down to the beach, but to complete the walk turn left up the valley to the church of St Levan. Inside there are very interesting 15th-century bench ends of court jesters and St James' pilgrims. From here cross the bend in the road and strike left over a stream and up a track past the backs of two long low granite cottages. Walk up the left side of the field ahead and over a stile. Keep to the left of the next field and cross another stile about half way up into a third field. Turn right over this to reach a third stile and then keep to the left-hand sides of two further fields. You now meet a track which leads to Roskestal Farm (if you miss the stiles and use the gates between fields, this is the only building on the horizon).

The track leads out on to the road. Turn left here and where the road makes a sharp right turn head straight on down a track signposted Mordross. Follow it back down into the valley and turn right just before you reach a row of cottages and wend your way back down to Porthgwarra car park.

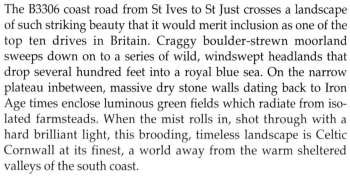

✪ NORTH COAST DRIVE

The B3306 coast road from St Ives to St Just crosses a landscape of such striking beauty that it would merit inclusion as one of the top ten drives in Britain. Craggy boulder-strewn moorland sweeps down on to a series of wild, windswept headlands that drop several hundred feet into a royal blue sea. On the narrow plateau inbetween, massive dry stone walls dating back to Iron Age times enclose luminous green fields which radiate from isolated farmsteads. When the mist rolls in, shot through with a hard brilliant light, this brooding, timeless landscape is Celtic Cornwall at its finest, a world away from the warm sheltered valleys of the south coast.

From St Ives the road runs between snaking walls of granite boulders, another beautiful scene unfolding at every turn. Turn off into the tiny village of **Zennor**, which shelters against the fiercesome storms in a hollow north of the road. The land here has been farmed since 2000BC and in the **Wayside Museum** (open daily Easter to end October, 10am-6pm) you can see and handle prehistoric stone mace heads and tools for digging, hammering and sharpening found in the area. There is also an interesting collection of rural bygones, tin-mining equipment and a traditional Cornish kitchen. Most of the 5,000 items on display are from the parish.The mediaeval church of St Senara contains a bench-end depicting the Mermaid of Zennor.

The **Tinner's Arms** in Zennor is an atmospheric local pub serving St Austell ales and simple home-made food: lasagne, chicken pie, good salads and ploughman's lunches. In summer you can sit outside on a terrace which overlooks the valley.

Four miles further along the B3306, just before Morvah, turn left up a narrow lane, signposted Madron, if you are interested in seeing some important prehistoric sites. After a mile you will see a former chapel, now Men-an-Tol Studio, on the right. Park in the lay-by here and take the footpath on the left. After 20 minutes, a stile on the right leads to **Men-an-Tol**. This upright holed stone has long been used for healing rituals and many svelte visitors still climb through it for luck and good health. Rejoin the footpath and walk a further mile or so to Carn Galver, a ridge off to the left. The walk to the summit is particularly appealing on a clear day when there are fabulous views over both coasts.

Bench ends at St Levan church

Another interesting site is **Chûn Castle**, a massive Iron Age hillfort. To reach it drive up the lane beside Men-an-Tol Studio and park beside Trehyllys Farm. Take the path to the right past a white boulder and clamber up to the dry stone castle walls. These have been much depleted for building material, but you can still appreciate the scale of the place and there are magnificent coastal views. Chûn Quiot, to the west, is the best preserved of the ancient burial chambers that litter the area. Even in high summer few tourists venture on to these moors and with the aid of Ian Cooke's excellent guide *Journey to the Stones*, you could spend an interesting day discovering prehistoric Cornwall.

Levant Beam Engine at Pendeen on the north coast

Back on the main coast road evidence of centuries of tin and copper mining lies all around, the long-abandoned engine houses and chimneys as much a part of the landscape as the farmsteads. For a closer view turn right off the coastal road at Pendeen and follow signs for the **Levant Beam Engine**. Perched dramatically on the edge of a cliff, this is the only Cornish beam engine operated by steam preserved on its original site. Built about 1840 to raise ore from the deep levels of the mine, its machinery has been painstakingly restored by the Trevithick Society and can be seen in action during the summer.

Opening times: 11am-4pm Sun and Mon over Easter, May and Spring Bank Hols; Fri and Sun during June; Sun-Fri Jul 1-Sept 12
Admission: adult £2; Child £1; NT members free

Nearby **St Just** is a charming little mining town of neat granite houses with a strong personality. It remains unspoilt by tourism, despite its proximity to Land's End, and at its centre is a grass-covered amphitheatre where mediaeval miracle plays were once performed.

PARADISE PARK

Over 240 species of British and migratory birds have been sighted in the Hayle estuary but on its bank is a wildlife park containing even more exotic species. Paradise Park is the home of the World Parrot Trust, dedicated to saving some of the 30 endangered species of parrot, as well as other rare rainforest birds. Over 80 different species have been successfully bred here and a visit is both entertaining and educational.

The large aviaries stand in the attractive landscaped grounds and each contains several species of birds who get along with one another. (The park tries to have at least three breeding pairs of each species.) As well as the brilliantly coloured parrots, there are scarlet and hyacinth macaws, rhinocerous hornbills from Borneo, toucans and noisy mynah birds. Female visitors will be treated to wolf-whistles from some of the more mischievous residents. In the largest aviary, which is 150ft long, you can watch some of the birds in flight, getting fit for the breeding season. Cranes are another speciality of the park including the elegant crowned cranes from south-east Africa. Information boards provide good explanations of where each bird is from, its behaviour and how successfully it has bred in the park. If you have children, ask for a copy of Professor Parrot's Spotter Guide to make the visit more fun.

There are also more familiar birds: golden and bald eagles, grey and barn owls, pheasants and starlings. From Easter to the end of September you can watch flying displays of eagles and falcons at noon and 3.30pm, weather permitting. Elsewhere there are Caribbean flamingos and endangered geese, pigeons and swans. There is also a farm park where children can meet and feed angora goats, donkeys, deer and pigs. The otter sanctuary contains European and Asian otters, and there are even endangered Humboldt penguins from Chile which are fed at 2.30pm each day.

Children who become bored with birdwatching can visit the adventure playground in the middle of the park with its sturdy climbing frames, rope ladders and tree house. There is also a barn containing video games and mechanical rides. A cafeteria serves snacks and refreshments and the park has its own pub, the Bird in Hand, across from the entrance for more substantial fare. The pub brews its own beer which you can see fermenting in the old stables.

Paradise Park, Hayle. Tel: 0736 757407
Opening times: daily all year, 10am-6pm (last admission 4pm)
Admission: adult £4.25; children 4-14 £2.25

☆ PENZANCE

Penzance has that laid-back, offbeat atmosphere of a place at the end of the line. In the town centre, hippies and genuine 'New Age' enthusiasts rub shoulders with local housewives out shopping. There are buskers on street corners and shops selling energising crystals and palmistry handbooks, flowing ethnic gear and joss sticks, and organic vegetarian snacks - everything the modern designer hippy could wish for.

Regency Square, Penzance

It is a pleasant town to wander around and worth a visit if the weather is unseasonable. Fine Georgian and Regency terraces and squares climb away from Mounts Bay, the legacy of the town's time as a fashionable watering hole. A cross-section of this architectural heritage can be seen in Chapel Street including the Egyptian House and the old Assembly Rooms in the Union Hotel. There are a number of interesting specialist shops including the Stencilled House, a former customs house whose interior has been beautifully decorated by Lyn Le Grice as a showplace for her intricately patterned stencils. The **Tourist Information Centre** is on Station Road; tel: 0736 62207.

> **The Turk's Head** in Chapel Street is the place to head for lunch. Its low beamed bars are below street level and as popular with locals as visitors. The menu is varied and the cooking excellent: warm baguettes filled with chilli and blue cheese, spicy chicken or roast beef and onion; chicken tikka, Chinese-style pork in ginger, and fresh lobster, crab, mussels and fisherman's pie. There is a separate cellar dining area and patio where children are allowed. Last orders: lunch 2.30pm; dinner 10pm.

Lighthouses have saved thousands of lives around the Cornish coast and Penzance is the site of the **Trinity House National Lifeboat Centre**, housed in a former buoy servicing yard. The exhibition starts with an 8-minute video on the history of lighthouses from the first Eddystone lighthouse, built in 1698, which was lit by candles to the sophisticated automated lighthouses and vessels in use today. There is an impressive collection of lighthouse optics and their mechanics, and former lighthouse keepers and engineers to explain how these worked. A replica kitchen and living room complete with curved furniture shows the cramped conditions of rock lighthouses.

Trinity House National Lighthouse Centre, Wharf Road (at the foot of Chapel Street), Penzance. Tel: 0736 60077
Opening times: daily Mar-Oct, 11am-5pm
Admission: adult £2; children 5-16 £1

If you are a keen museum-goer, **Penlee House Museum** is worth popping into. It is a rather fusty place in need of a more modern look, but as well as the usual domestic bygones, neolithic artefacts and old photographs and posters of Penzance's heyday as a resort, it contains an important collection of paintings from the Newlyn School. The fishing port of Newlyn is an extension of Penzance today, but in the late 19th century it was described by the father of the School, Stanhope Forbes, as 'a sort of English Concarneau' and artists flocked here to work in the open air, producing some evocative paintings of community life.

Penzance and District Museum, Penlee House, Morrab Road. Tel: 0736 63625
Opening times: all year Mon-Fri 10.30am-4.30pm; Sat 10.30am-12.30pm
Admission: small charge in summer

ST IVES

The extraordinary intensity and clarity of the light in St Ives lends it a distinctly Mediterranean feel. There is a film-set quality about its scenery: the aesthetically pleasing jumble of white-washed and slate-hung cottages climbing away from the fishing harbour; the white sands, palms and cypresses of sun-drenched Porthminster Beach so reminiscent of the old French Riviera, and the heavy surf and salt-laden winds of Porthmeor Beach on the wild north coast. Such contrasting scenes and moods, all within a few minutes' walk of each other, hold the key to St Ives' enduring popularity with artists and visitors.

The fishing harbour of St Ives

In July and August St Ives can become so crowded that you may fail to appreciate its charm, but outside these busy months it still weaves its spell over visitors. Behind the harbour the warren of alleys and tiny squares of Downalong, the old fishermen's quarter, remain full of character and thread up past neat terraced rows of miners' cottages to 'The Island', a green mound topped by the tiny chapel of St Nicholas which is a popular spot for bird-watching. St Ives offers sheltered beaches whatever the direction of the wind: surfers head for Porthmeor, while families prefer Porthminster south of the harbour. Don't even think of driving through the centre of town; the narrow winding streets are tricky to negotiate and there are very few parking spaces. From the main car parks it is a 10-minute downhill walk to the harbour front. The **Tourist Information Centre** is in the Guildhall, Street-an-Pol; tel: 0736 796297.

In the late 19th century, artists from all over the world flocked to St Ives in the wake of Whistler and Sickert, to capture on canvas its special light, ever-changing seascapes, and traditional fishing and mining communities at work and play. Ben Nicholson, Peter Lanyon and Barbara Hepworth headed a new wave in the 1940s, and today you come across artist's studios at every turn, many converted from former sail lofts, especially along Porthmeor Beach. *Art about St Ives*, available in local bookshops, is an excellent guide to the artistic legacy of St Ives, and tells you where to locate paintings, sculptures and galleries as well as places of interest connected with the artists' colony past and present.

The **Barbara Hepworth Museum** is housed in the sculptress's former home and studio (she died here in a fire in 1972) and is well worth a visit. The ground floor displays tell the story of her life with photographs and interesting hand-written essays on art and the influence of the area's landscape on her work. Upstairs her former sitting room and bedroom contains some of the original furnishings and a selection of her smaller wood and stone carvings. But the highlight of the museum is the sculpture garden. When Hepworth began to work in bronze in 1958 she often kept back an artist's cast of each new sculpture for the garden. There are 18 bronzes and three large stone carvings and in her workshop alongside, untouched since her death, are plaster moulds and an unfinished work in marble. Hepworth was concerned with 'the essential quality of light in relation to sculpture' and new ways of 'piercing the form to contain colour' and the sculptures in the garden illustrate these ideas brilliantly.

The Barbara Hepworth Museum, turn left on Fore Street by the Union Inn.
Tel: 0736 796226
Opening times: Jul and Aug, Mon-Sat 10am-6.30pm, Sun 2-6pm; rest of year, Mon-Sat 10am-5.30pm (4.30pm in winter), closed Sun
Admission: adult 50p; child 25p

Hepworth Museum Sculpture Garden, St Ives

There is a great deal of indifferent art on sale in St Ives. A good selection of the best art and craft work can be found in two galleries. The **Wills Lane Gallery** (open Monday-Saturday 10am-1pm) is owned by Henry Gilbert, an architect who became a good friend of Barbara Hepworth. He specialises in works by leading contemporary artists, including some affordable tactile sculptures in serpentine. On Fore Street, the **New Craftsman** (open Monday-Friday 9am-5.30pm; Saturday 10am-5pm) has something of everything, from expensive bronzes and pottery to imaginative jewellery and captivating wooden cats.

Behind the harbour in a former Seamen's Mission, the **St Ives Museum** is one of the largest and most interesting of the county's local museums - an Aladdin's cave of bygones, seafaring paraphernalia, old costumes, children's toys and all kinds of railway, fishing and tin-mining memorabilia. Of particular interest are the beautiful models of sailing and steam ships and photographs of wrecks on the Cornish coast by the Victorian photographer Gibson. Downstairs there is more early camera work showing St Ives in the 1880s and the flurry of activity surrounding a pilchard catch in Polperro.

The St Ives Museum, turn left at Smeaton's Pier. Tel: 0736 796005
Opening times: Easter-first week Oct, 10am-4pm
Admission: adults 50p; children 25p

The eagerly awaited **Tate Gallery St Ives** is scheduled to open Easter 1993 in a building facing Porthmeor Beach which has been designed by Evans & Shalev, architects of the award-winning Truro Law Courts. Its aim is to show the achievements of artists associated with St Ives from 1920 to 1975. The five galleries will display changing groups of work - paintings, drawings, sculptures, prints and ceramics - from the Tate Gallery's collection supplemented by loans including works by Ben Nicholson, Patrick Heron, Alfred Wallis and Bryan Wynter as well as the ceramics of Bernard Leach. (The Leach Pottery on the road out to Zennor currently contains a display of his Japanese-inspired hand-thrown stoneware and porcelain.)

☆ ## ST MICHAEL'S MOUNT

For two hours each side of low tide you can walk across a causeway from Marazion to this castle-topped granite crag which rises so dramatically from Mounts Bay. Otherwise park in one of the car parks and island ferrymen will take you across for a small fee. There has been a port here since at least the Iron Age when tin was traded with the continent, and the homes of the Mount's boatmen and fishermen still line the quay. Across from the ticket office a small cinema screens a 15-minute film on the Mount's long history as a Celtic shrine, Benedictine monastery, military garrison, and, since the 17th century, the private home of the St Aubyn Family.

The climb up to the castle itself is quite strenuous and not recommended for people with heart or respiratory conditions. At the entrance Walkman self-guided tours are available and it is well worth paying the extra £1. Far preferable to digging around in a guidebook, the 45-minute audio tour brings the rooms to life, mixing the commentary with evocative sound effects: the furious noise of battle, Renaissance music, and an 18th-century dinner party at full throttle. The interior is surprisingly cosy and small-scale, a mix of 12th- to 19th-century styles which blend harmoniously together.

St Michael's Mount rising from Mounts Bay

There are magnificent views over the coast from the different terraces which also provide a closer look at the private terraced gardens which tumble down the cliffside and include 18th-century walled gardens. These are open to the public during April and May only. The tour finishes in a small museum containing some intricately embroidered 18th-century court costumes and a model of the Mount made from Champagne corks by a former butler.

St Michael's Mount, Marazion. Tel: 0736 710507
Opening times: Apr 1-end Oct, Mon-Fri 10.30am-5.45pm (last admission 4.45pm)
Admission: adult £3; child £1.50; NT members free

☆ TREGWAINTON GARDEN

At the foot of granite hills behind Penzance, Tregwainton is particularly noted for its very tender rhododendrons from Assam and Upper Burma, raised from seedlings in the 1920s when most of the planting was done. It is a long, narrow garden straddling the course of a stream, and is of particular interest to knowledgeable gardeners who will appreciate the great success with which tender exotics have been raised here.

April is the very best time to see Tregwainton in its spring glory, although there is plenty of colour here from March, when some rather special magnolias flower, until the end of September when the stream disappears under a blaze of blue hydrangeas. Of particular interest are the walled gardens whose brick walls and unusual sloping beds were designed to trap the sun's heat. They were built in the 1820s to grow early vegetables, but now contain some of the garden's finest magnolias, evergreens, and particularly tender Asian plants. The house is not open to the public but from the lawn in front of it there is a fine view of St Michael's Mount through an arch of trees. No refreshments.

Tregwainton Garden, Madron (signposted off the A3071 Penzance-St Just road).
Tel: 0736 63021
Opening times: Mar 1-end Oct, Wednes-Sat and Bank Hol Mons, 10.30am-5.30pm
Admission: adult £2.40; child £1.20; NT members free

WHERE TO STAY

Botallack

♿ ✉ £ ☂

Manor Farm, *Botallack, St Just*
TR19 7QG
Tel: 0736 788525
Open all year
Joyce Cargeeg offers a warm Cornish welcome at her 300-year-old farmhouse on the rugged north coast. It oozes character and is filled with period and Chinese antiques, old oils and prints, and featured as Nampara in the television series Poldark. There are three cosy bedrooms upstairs, all with their own bathrooms; a lovely breakfast room with its original wooden ceiling and huge granite fireplace, and a sitting room for guests. Joyce is a mine of information on the area.

Penzance

⌂ ▭ £££ ⅄5

The Abbey Hotel, *Abbey Street,*
Penzance TR18 4AR
Tel: 0736 66906
Closed 2 wks Jan
This striking 17th-century house has
been turned into a delightful small
hotel by Michael and Jean Cox. The
decor throughout is highly original
and rooms are furnished with well-
chosen antiques and all kinds of
interesting ethnic artefacts. The sitting room invites you to curl up and
read a good book or relax with an
after-dinner drink. There are seven
bedrooms, and those at the front
have fine views over Penzance harbour. The set dinner menu offers
good French cooking.

Porthcurno

⌂ ▭ ££ ⅄8

Mariners Lodge Hotel, *Porthcurno,*
near Penzance
Tel: 0736 810236
Open all year
What marks this hotel out is its
splendid position on a headland
above Porthcurno Beach and just a
few minutes' walk from the Minack
Theatre. The 11 bedrooms are simply
decorated, some with en suite bathrooms and large private sea-view terraces. Theatre suppers are served in
the dining room at 5pm; later there's
a bistro menu regularly featuring
sole, steak and noisettes of lamb.

St Hilary

⌂ ✉ ££ ⅄

Enny's Farm, *St Hilary, Penzance*
TR20 9BZ
Tel: 0736 740262
Closed Nov
Sue White's farmhouse is the epito-
me of country living. Set in a lovely
garden with a grass tennis court and
a swimming pool, Enny's is a wonderfully atmospheric 17th-century
manor on its own near the river
Hayle. There are three large stylish
bedrooms, two with four-posters, all
en suite; and two family suites in a
converted barn next door.

What makes this a really special
place is the warm relaxing atmosphere and the excellent cooking.
Guests meet at 7pm and chat over a
sherry in the cosy sitting room before
tucking into an imaginative four-
course menu: fresh fish and seafood,
game in season, and home-made
bread, croissants and ice-cream.

St Ives

⌂ ✗ 🐕 ▭ £££ ⅄

Pedn-Olva Hotel, *Porthminster Beach,*
St Ives TR26 2EA
Tel: 0736 796222
Open all year
The location of this family-run hotel
could not be more perfect. From the
bar there is a picture postcard view
of St Ives harbour and from the dining room a panorama of Porthminster Beach. Sunbathing terraces,
one with a small pool, have been
built out over the rocks and steps
lead down to the beach. All the 35
prettily decorated rooms have sea
views. The restaurant specialises in
fresh fish and seafood and home-
made fare is available in the bar at
lunchtimes. Last orders: bar lunch
2.30; dinner 10pm (earlier in winter).

WHERE TO EAT

Penzance
✗ ▭ ££ ☂

The Hungry Horse, *Old Bakehouse Lane, off Chapel Street, Penzance*
Tel: 0736 63446
Dinner only; closed Sun except Jul - mid-Sept
This cosy, friendly restaurant in an old bakery is very popular with local residents and offers particularly good value for money. It specialises in charcoal grilled Aberdeen Angus steaks which have been naturally reared, together with kebabs, local fish and a wide selection of tasty freshly baked pizzas. Small wine list. Last orders for dinner 10pm.

St Ives
✗ ▭ £££

The Pig n' Fish, *Norway Lane, St Ives*
Tel: 0736 794204
Dinner only; open weekends in winter or on request
In this small, licensed retaurant, pop-ular with locals, the emphasis is on locally caught fish and shellfish, selected daily by chef, Paul Sellars. His eclectic menu has a Medi-terranean flavour with dishes such as bourride (a fish stew), crab tortilla with salsa and, in summer, a delicious raspberry and kir summer pudding. His partner, Debby Wilkins, does the serving. The bread is home-made and there are compli-mentary appetisers. Last orders for dinner 9pm.

St Ives
✗ ▭ ££ ☂

Russets, *Chapel Street, St Ives*
Tel: 0736 794700
Dinner only; closed Mon, Jan & 3 wks Feb
This simple bistro furnished with country wooden chairs and checked tablecloths serves some of the best no-frills fish and seafood in town and is a great favourite with locals. Crab claws with mayonnaise, Dover sole, John Dory and crawfish mornay are regulars on the menu, plus whatever the fishing boats bring in. It has no licence, but you can bring your own wine. Last orders for dinner 10pm.

Treen
🍽 🐕 ▭ £ ☂

Logan Rock Inn, *Treen, near Porthcurno*
Tel: 0736 810495
Open all year
This pub takes it name from an extra-ordinary boulder perched on the cliff-top a short walk from the vil-lage. The main bar is a welcoming place with a low beamed ceiling, coal fire and traditional high-backed set-tles. Children are allowed in the fam-ily room and restaurant area, and in summer trestle tables are set out in the front courtyard. The food, ordered through a hatch leading to the kitchen, is very good with some unusual fish and vegetarian pies with cheese crumble tops, fresh crab sandwiches, seafood pasta and char-coal-grilled steaks. Last orders: lunch 2.30pm; dinner 9pm.

THE NORTH COAST FROM NEWQUAY TO PADSTOW

The beaches along this stretch of the north coast are magnificent, from long strands pounded by surf to sheltered funnel-shaped coves which are perfect for families. John Betjeman spent his childhood holidays in Trebetherick, across the Camel from Padstow, and grew to love this area of Cornwall. In his poem *Delectable Duchy* he sings its praises:

Those golden and unpeopled bays,
The shadowy cliffs and sheep-worn ways,
The white unpopulated surf,
The thyme- and mushroom-scented turf,
The slate-hung farms, the oil-lit chapels,
Thin elms and lemon-coloured apples...

The bays can become very crowded with holidaymakers nowadays, but out of season and towards sunset the beaches bordering the Camel estuary and Constantine Bay remain glorious tranquil places for an evening stroll. A little cultural diversion can be found in a clutch of historic homes open to the public: Prideaux Place in Padstow, Pencarrow near Bodmin and Trerice behind Newquay.

If you are travelling with energetic children, a cycle ride should send them early to bed. The Camel Trail, a cycling and walking path following the course of the River Camel, passes through beautiful scenery and all kinds of bicycles, and even trailers for babies, can be hired in Padstow, Bodmin or Wadebridge. Dairyland Farm World, an excellent farm park built around a working dairy farm near Newquay, is another popular family attraction where you could spend the best part of a day.

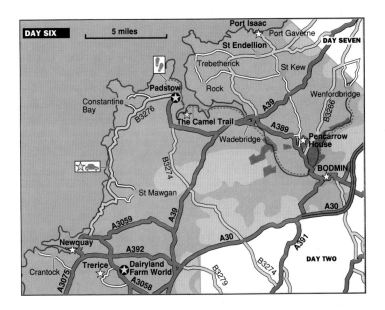

☆ BODMIN

Bodmin lies at the geographical centre of Cornwall but despite its long history as an important Cornish market town and, for a period, the county town, there is not a great deal to see: a fine 15th-century church, all the usual High Street shops, and several small museums including a collection of steam locomotives undergoing restoration at Bodmin Station from where you can take steam train rides in summer. The **Tourist Information Centre** for the area is at Shire House in Mount Folly Square above the parish church (tel: 0208 76616). Enclosed by hills, Bodmin can seem rather a dark, bleak place, especially on a dull day, and you may prefer to stick to the coast. However, there are two attractions of some interest.

Old Bodmin Gaol, built in 1778 as the county prison, was seen as a model prison in its time. During the First World War, the Crown Jewels and the Domesday Book were among the British treasures stored within its impregnable stone walls. Inside are several floors of dank, gloomy cells which today contain life-size tableaux depicting the evil deeds of some of the gaol's most infamous inhabitants. Although the papier-maché tableaux look somewhat frayed around the edges, they do give young children a scare and some are really quite gory: men strangling women or hacking them to death and skeletons slumped in corners. Boards tell the story behind the murders, and there are copies of crime reports from the *West Britain* newspaper which give a good idea of how desperate Victorian times were for the poor, with people being hanged for stealing clothing and imprisoned for stealing milk from a cow. It is worth buying a guide to the history of the gaol as you go in as this is not covered in detail inside. You exit through a tea room and licensed bar.

Bodmin Gaol, Berrycombe Road, Bodmin. Tel: 0208 76292
Opening times: daily Easter-mid Oct 10am-5.30pm
Admission: adult £2.80; children over 5 £1.40

If you are interested in war memorabilia pay a visit to the **Duke of Cornwall's Light Infantry Regimental Museum**. The regiment, raised in 1702, has taken part in many of Britain's most famous campaigns: the American War of Independence, the Battle of Waterloo, the Crimea and the World Wars. Arranged in several large rooms are visual displays of the different campaigns with good clear explanations of what happened, supported by memorabilia, uniforms, weaponry and personal effects. Among them is a patchwork counterpane made during the Siege of Lucknow from the scarlet jackets and blue trousers of dead soldiers and green baize from the Residency billiard table. The collections of guns, revolvers and medals, orders and decorations are exceptional.

The Regimental Museum, The Keep, opposite Bodmin General Station.
Tel: 0208 72810
Opening times: Mon-Fri 8am-5pm; closed weekends and public hols
Admission: adult £1; child 50p

Just outside Bodmin, the **Candle Shop** on the A389 Bodmin-Wadebridge road sells a large range of quality candles, candle holders and candle-making materials. These include life-size owls, ducks, small dogs, and cats which are realistic enough to elicit a few barks from short-sighted dogs. They will also make candles in specific shades to order. The shop is open 10am-6pm on weekdays all year; Saturday and Sunday from Easter-end September.

☆ THE CAMEL TRAIL

The Camel Trail is an 18-mile walking, cycling and riding path running alongside the river Camel on disused railway lines. This imaginative tourist development is owned and managed by the district council and the fairly level trail passes through delightful scenery, from Padstow on the coast, inland to Wadebridge, Bodmin and Wenfordbridge. It is very popular with cyclists, especially in summer, and bicycles of all shapes and sizes can be hired, including tandems, children's trikes, and even trailers for babies which can be adapted to take a carry-cot or child car seat.

The 5-mile Padstow-Wadebridge stretch of the trail is the most visually appealing and the most popular. On fine summer days you may feel frustrated trying to walk or cycle here as it can become very crowded. Starting from the car park on Padstow's harbourfront, the wide gravel trail hugs the bank of the Camel estuary. At low tide shallow channels curl around the sand flats attracting a rich variety of wading birds and wild fowl: herons, cormorants, oyster catchers, terns and teals among them. Ahead Bodmin Moor rises from woodlands like a beacon before you reach Wadebridge town centre.

If you feel the need of a windcheater or walking boots, **Country Wise** at 27 Molesworth Street (the main street through Wadebridge) is one of the best outdoor clothes and equipment shops in Cornwall with a large selection of the latest gear.

From Wadebridge to Bodmin the trail follows the line of one of the world's first steam railways. Opened in 1834, it was originally built to carry sea-sand from the Camel estuary to sweeten the acidic farmland inland, the trains returning with granite and china clay. You pick up this 5-mile trail at Wadebridge Station, now converted into the **John Betjeman Centre**, a day centre for the elderly containing a Betjeman memorabilia room with some of his letters, hand-written poems and personal belongings. At 11am and 3pm *First and Last Love*, a television documentary about Betjeman in Cornwall, is shown. The centre is open 10am-noon, 2-4.30pm except Sundays.

This section of the trail is a land of marsh and water meadow full of yellow iris in early summer. Gradually the valley narrows and ancient woodlands shade the path: **Gaff and Undertown Woods**, about two miles along this stretch, are open to the public. In summer, refreshments are served in a tea garden overlooking the river just before Boscarne Junction. From here you can choose either to climb up the hill into Bodmin or continue along the banks of the Camel to Poley's Bridge.

> There is **good fishing** on the upper reaches of the Camel, con-trolled by the Wadebridge Angling Association between Wadebridge and Grogley. The game fish season is from mid-May to mid-December. Salmon are plentiful and, between June and late August, sea trout. Day permits are available from local tackle shops. In addition you will need to purchase a National River Authority permit available from any NRA office; the near-est is found in Victoria Square, Bodmin. Tel: 0208 78301.

On this final 6-mile stretch tall beech trees shade the path and lean out across the river as it tumbles over a series of salmon weirs. Where the trail crosses the busy A389 just outside Bodmin, the **Borough Arms**, a couple of hundred yards uphill on the right, is full of railway memorabilia and serves filling bar meals and good beer. This tranquil section of the trail is less used and there are some lovely picnic spots on the riverbank. At **Helland Bridge** turn left to see one of Cornwall's finest mediae-val bridges, and at Poley's Bridge go out through the car park to visit an interesting pottery, founded at **Wenfordbridge** by Michael Cardew, who studied under Bernard Leach in St Ives. There is a small museum of early 20th-century pots collected by Cardew.

Bicycles can be hired throughout the year; in July and August you will need to reserve several days in advance. Rates vary from £4 for touring bikes to £10 for the latest mountain bikes. Padstow: Glyn Davis, 300yds upstream from the riverside town car park. Tel: 0841 532594. Wadebridge: Bridge Bike Hire, across from Molesworth St car park. Tel: 0208 81305. Bodmin: Bodmin Trading Company, Church Square. Tel: 0208 72557

DAIRYLAND FARM WORLD

Farm parks are mushrooming all over Britain, but Cornwall contains the first - and possibly the best - farm diversification of this kind. There is a great deal to interest both adults and children and Dairyland very successfully combines education with entertainment. Set in a lovely rural landscape four miles from Newquay, the park is the creation of Rex Davey whose family farms 550-acre Tresillian Barton. When the Daveys installed a high-tech rotary milking parlour in 1973 it aroused such interest that they decided to open it to the public together with Mr Davey's personal collection of rural bygones. Today there is also an extensive farm animal park, an excellent nature trail, and some interesting play equipment, designed and built at Dairyland.

The highlight for most visitors is the American 'merry-go-round' milking parlour which cost £100,000 to install, an investment

Merry-go-round milking parlour at Dairyland Farm World

which no dairy farmer could afford today . The black-and-white Friesian cows enter the parlour and step on to a revolving platform where they are locked automatically into a yoke, fed from a manger, and milked to the sound of classical music. Once they have completed a revolution on the turntable milking time is over and they are automatically released back into the yard. Milking takes place between 3 and 4.45pm every day. The building also contains a large exhibition with clear explanations of the milking process and all sorts of interesting facts and figures about dairy farming, from the history of the cow from 2000BC to how much a cow is worth today.

The Country Life Museum displays thousands of artefacts amassed by Rex Davey since the Forties. This is not the usual haphazard collection of bygones but a series of appealing sets showing rural Cornwall as it was a century or more ago. The displays depict the work of the farmer, his wife, the miller, wheelwright, saddler, and even the undertaker, with good, clear background explanations. It is very much a hands-on museum and - except for the poachers' traps - visitors can handle all the tools and implements. There are also working models of traditional farm machinery and a water garden containing models of water-powered machines.

Children particularly enjoy visiting the farm animals in the paddocks and the indoor animal ark. They can help feed lambs and kids, and visit the calf nursery where calves are fed at 1.30pm in spring and summer. There are all kinds of imaginative play things too: straw houses to clamber around, sand pits with farm-designed diggers and see-saws, an adventure playground and, for older children, an assault course.

Do not miss the nature trail, a 30-minute walk through the farm's nature reserve. Everything is labelled, even common trees and hedgerow plants, and there are ponds full of trout which you can feed. You can bring your own picnic to eat in the walled garden or have lunch in the café. The farm shop sells fresh produce, including delicious unpasteurised milk. Expect to spend around 4 hours in the park if you want to see everything.

Dairyland Farm World, on the A 3058 north of Summercourt. Tel: 0872 510246
Opening times: daily early Apr-late Oct 10.30am-5.30pm (noon-5pm Apr and Oct)
Admission: adult £3.95; child 3-15 £2.95

☆ NEWQUAY

Newquay is Cornwall's largest seaside resort but sadly it is showing its age. Like so many English resorts it has been a victim of the growth in foreign holidays and has little else to offer other than sand and surf. The streets are lined with cheap souvenir shops, paint peels from the stucco-fronted hotels and it has that faintly depressing air of a place just keeping its head above water. The town only really comes alive during July and August, but if you are touring Cornwall the traffic jams and parking hassles during this period make it a place to avoid.

That said, Newquay does have fabulous beaches backed by high brown slate cliffs, and it is famous as a surfing resort. In June or late September the wide beaches are lovely to stroll along and there are always dozens of surfers riding the awesome waves. The best time to see them in action is just after low tide. Fistral is reckoned to have the finest surfing, while Town Beach is the safest for families and swimmers. Lifeguards are on duty in summer.

> If you prefer to relax on a secluded beach, head for **Porth Joke** just west of Newquay. From the A3075 take the road signposted Crantock, pass through the village to West Pentire where you will find a car park in a field to the left at the end of the road. From here it's a 10-minute walk along a footpath (signposted Vugga Cove, then Polly Joke) to a lovely funnel-shaped beach below glistening black cliffs. There are no toilets or refreshments on the beach.

 Newquay Zoo is a popular attraction. While it carefully promotes its conservation role, one cannot help but feel sorry for the grouchy black bears and bored lions. Hens, ducks and geese wander around freely and children will enjoy exploring the warren, usually filled with baby rabbits. It stands in 8 acres of well landscaped grounds and there are good explanations of where the animals come from, their habits and diet but, unless you have children, give it a miss. Opposite the zoo is an undercover water park with a smallish lagoon pool, water slides and plenty of seating space - but it's not large enough to cope with the crowds on a rainy summer's day.

Newquay Zoo, off the A3075 through town. Tel: 0637 873342
Opening times: daily Easter-end Oct 10am-5pm (last admission 4pm)
Admission: adult £3.95; child 5-16 £2.40, under 5 £1

☆ NEWQUAY-PADSTOW COAST DRIVE

This roller-coaster drive, dipping down to the water's edge before climbing back on to the cliffs again, affords beautiful coastal panoramas. Take the B3276 from Newquay and look back to see the best of the resort: the beautiful sands, the cliff-top Victorian terraces and, of course, the magnificent rollers full of wet-suited figures. After Watergate Bay the road dips down to Mawgan Porth. Immediately after crossing the bridge turn right to St Mawgan.

Bonsai Nursery in St Mawgan   *Bedruthan Steps*

The pretty village of St Mawgan is the home of the **Bonsai Nursery** containing Robert Hore's exquisite collection of bonsai trees. Some of these miniature trees are over a century old, lovingly shaped and pruned to resemble their full-grown relatives in all but size. There are over 50 species including Chinese red maples, junipers, elms, beeches and even Virginia creeper and bamboo. Many are for sale and the shop sells specialist equipment, pots and books on the Japanese art of bonsai. The nursery is open every day all year from 10am-6pm; tel: 0637 860116.

From St Mawgan rejoin the coast road again and, after a mile or so, turn off for **Bedruthan Steps**. Like Kynance Cove on the

Lizard this is cliff erosion at its finest; the sea foaming and swirling around great stacks and arches, long separated from the contorted slate cliffs. The bay is particularly impressive around low tide and towards sunset when the stacks stand in pools of brilliant green water along the sandy beach. At present there is no access down to the beach (which is too dangerous for swimming) as dangerous fissures have been found near the cliff staircase. Instead walk to the other end of the bay to view the scene from a completely different perspective. There is a good National Trust café beside the car park serving snacks, home-made cakes and ice-creams until 5.15pm.

Three miles further on turn left to reach **Constantine Bay**, one of the finest beaches in Cornwall. With its golf course and smart detached homes, Constantine attracts the well heeled. There is parking for only a dozen cars alongside the beach, but in summer fields are opened to cope with the visitors. The dune-backed beach has been left in its natural state and beyond the fine sands there are large rock pools with sandy bottoms which children adore. The beach faces west so it can be uncomfortable if the wind is blowing from that direction; bathing can also be dangerous then too. Should this be the case, head instead for Padstow's more sheltered east-facing beaches, a 10-minute drive away.

Constantine Bay, one of Cornwall's finest beaches

Prideaux Place, Padstow

 ## PADSTOW

In 1602 Cornish chronicler Richard Carew described Padstow as 'a town and haven of suitable quality, for both are the best that the north Cornish coast possesseth'. This statement remains as true today as it was in Elizabethan times. In contrast to many Cornish resorts, you will be hard pressed to find candy floss and chip shops here. Instead there are art galleries, smart cake shops and delicatessens in pretty streets lined with slate-hung and pastel-coloured houses. The trading ships may have gone, but the town still supports an active fishing fleet and you can watch the boats unload on the quay, from where boat trips along the beautiful beach-lined Camel estuary depart.

> **Stein's deli** in Middle Street is just the place to put together a beach picnic. The home-made pasties are among the best in Cornwall and more exotic fare includes mussels stuffed with garlic butter, duck terrine with pistachios and fish pie - all made in the kitchens of the excellent Seafood Restaurant. Wine and Champagne are also sold here.

Standing in wooded grounds above the town is **Prideaux Place**, home of the Prideaux-Brune family since 1592. It still retains its classic Elizabethan E-shaped façade but the interior has the feel of a comfortable home of Jane Austen's time. The 45-minute guided tour is taken by one of two local ladies who are both full of enthusiasm for their subject, bringing this ancient family seat and its occupants to life with tales of adventure and intrigue, and the curious things being unmasked as restoration takes place. It is so refreshing to meet guides who can entertain those with no more than a passing interest in historic homes, presenting a complete contrast to the cold formality found in some National Trust-owned properties.

London barrister Peter Prideaux-Brune inherited the house from his reclusive father in 1988 by which time it had fallen into considerable disrepair. The elegant reception rooms, all used by the family, have since been restored with great sensitivity and taste and are full of interesting family heirlooms and particularly fine china. The original great hall has long since been divided in half. On the ground floor there is a handsome 17th-century panelled dining room, while in the gallery above is the original 16th-century ceiling, a plaster bas-relief of the biblical story of Susannah and the Elders which was hidden by a false ceiling until recently. Of the house's 81 rooms, 44 are bedrooms but only six are habitable; the rest are as the American Army left them at the end of the Second World War, complete with such notices as Lance Sergeant's Mess.

Prideaux Place, Padstow. Tel: 0841 532411
Opening times: 1.30-5pm Sun-Thurs May 24-Sept 30, Whitsun and Aug Bank Hols,
and from Easter Sat for two weeks
Admission: adult £3; child £1.50

PADSTOW BEACH WALK

There is no modern bungalow rash around Padstow; a 10-minute walk from the harbour brings you into open countryside. This 90-minute circular walk starts from the quay, but you can do it the other way round leaving from Prideaux Place. Walk around the harbour and up a short lane into a park to pick up the coastal footpath. There are plenty of benches from which to admire the constantly changing ratios of sea and sand in the estuary. Before long you pass a lovely sheltered sandy cove, perfect for sunbathing, and soon after the whole of Padstow Bay is spread out before you. Carry on half-way around Harbour Cove, another beautiful stretch of creamy sand backed by dunes, before turning inland. Climb over two slate stiles to reach Sand Lane. Turn left here and walk along the lane past Tregirls Farm and Prideaux Place, from where you can wend your way back down to the harbour again.

The resort of **Rock**, a popular sailing centre, lies opposite Padstow and a small passenger ferry connects them. As with Trebetherick to the north, where Sir John Betjeman spent his childhood holidays, Rock has seen a great deal of modern development. However, there's a beautiful walk through the dunes beside the golf course or, at low tide, along the sand flats to **St Enodoc Church** with its crooked granite spire. The tiny church was once buried beneath the sand, now kept out by a tamarisk-covered wall, and the churchyard contains the graves of John Betjeman and his mother. Try to arrive here late in the day when the beauty and tranquillity of the scene is heightened. As the fishing boats cut through the estuary, seagulls in their wake, and the setting sun casts a golden glow over the beaches you will see why John Betjeman so loved this place.

☆ PENCARROW HOUSE

The magnificent mile-long drive up to this handsome Georgian house is a real scene-setter. It was laid out in the 1840s and a number of the original trees survive, including hugely layered Japanese cedars and *Araucaria araucana* which acquired their common name of 'Monkey Puzzle' at Pencarrow after a guest commented that they would puzzle a monkey. Through the trees there are tantalising glimpses of the beautiful park and woodland that surround the house.

The Pencarrow estate has been owned by the Molesworth family and their descendants, the Molesworth-St Aubyns, since Elizabethan times and the house, built in the 1770s, is the 15th baronet's main residence today. For lovers of portraiture, Chinese porcelain, and 18th-century antiques, Pencarrow is full of interest. The 30-minute guided tour takes you through a succession of elegant reception rooms, a couple of bedrooms and the nursery. The music room is particularly lovely with its rococo ceiling depicting the four seasons and maple panelling decorated with fine mouldings of birds, fruit and flowers.

Throughout the house there are attractive 19th-century furnishing fabrics, several of which have been copied by textile manufacturer Bakers of London and re-issued. They include a delicate 19th-century Chinese linen, patterned with a bamboo and bird design, recently rediscovered under several layers of wallpaper. The family portraits are particularly fine and include a possibly unrivalled series by Sir Joshua Reynolds. Upstairs the Corner Bedroom is the one probably occupied by Sir Arthur Sullivan who composed the music for that fairytale of the aristocracy, *Iolanthe*, while staying here.

The park surrounding the house is a delightful place for a stroll and has always been known for its large collection of specimen conifers. The woodlands are particularly lovely in late spring and early summer when the many species of rhododendrons come into flower and bluebells carpet the woodlands, and again in autumn when the cockspur thorns and maples turn colour. In a courtyard behind the house there is a tea-room and a small children's play area, as well as another of the Cornwall Crafts Association's excellent galleries exhibiting and selling some of the best craftwork in the county, from carved bowls to hand-knitted jumpers. You can also pick your own soft fruit here in season.

Pencarrow House, Washaway, near Bodmin (signposted off the A389).
Tel: 0208 84369
Opening times: House and craft centre open Easter-mid Oct, Sun-Thurs 1.30-5pm
(June 1 - mid-Sept open from 11am); gardens open daily from dawn to dusk, Easter -
mid-Oct
Admission: adult £3; child 5-16 £1.50; garden only adult £1; child 50p

☆ PORT ISAAC

It seems incredible that cartloads of slate could ever have made it safely down the steep lanes leading to the harbour at Port Isaac, but until the coming of the railway slate from the important Delabole quarry was shipped through here. Although there is some parking on the beach, it is strongly advised to use the main car park above and walk down into this gem of a fishing village. Port Isaac remains pleasingly unspoilt, despite its increasing reliance on tourism. The slate-hung and white-washed cottages, shops and pubs are clustered on hillside ledges linked by steep alleys, some just the width of a man. From the pier, constructed in the reign of Henry VIII, you can watch the comings-and-goings of the lobster and crab fishermen. A new section of coastal path connecting Port Isaac with the hamlet of Portquin has been specially created by the National Trust. However, it is a very difficult walk with long steep flights of stairs following the contours of the cliff but it is worth doing the easier first section to admire the impressive cliffscape and Tintagel Castle to the north.

The harbour at Port Isaac

St Endellion lies a couple of miles south of Port Isaac and its handsome 15th-century church is the setting for two important music festivals which take place over Easter and during the last week of July and the first week of August. You can hear choral and chamber music as well as violin concertos and symphonies performed by visiting professional musicians. A few doors away is Glebe Farm Dairy which sells delicious home-made ice cream.

☆ TRERICE

Few Elizabethan and Jacobean manor houses have survived intact in Cornwall: Trerice is a rare exception. Half-hidden by trees, its curving grey gables command no distant view as Elizabethan builders cared more for sheltered places and the presence of spring water than for a wide prospect. It was the seat of the Arundells, an important Cornish family who built the manor and lived here for several generations before becoming absentee landlords and finally selling it. When the National Trust took it on in 1953 it was in a fairly poor state of repair, but many of its period features remained intact.

Visitors can walk freely around the house with guides in each room happy to answer questions and point out special features. Except for the great table in the Hall, Trerice contains no family furnishings and very few portraits. Instead the National Trust has brought together period pieces of West Country provenance where possible, including portraits of people the Arundells would have known as well as the Stuart kings whom the family supported during the Civil War. There are also several works by John Opie including a self-portrait. The highlight of Trerice is the Great Chamber, with a barrel-shaped plasterwork ceiling dating from 1572, its rich detailing unrestored and in excellent condition.

The gardens contain summer flowering plants, an orchard planted with old varieties of fruit trees, and a lovely rose garden created by one of the Trust's tenants. The great barn, thought to date from the 15th century, now contains a good Trust-run restaurant serving freshly cooked lunches, soups and salads from noon-2pm and cream teas from 2.30pm. Wine, cider and beer are available with meals. In the old stables there is a collection of lawnmowers showing the development of this essential English gardening tool over 150 years.

Trerice, signposted from the A3098 at Kestle Mill, 3 miles south of Newquay.
Tel: 0637 875404
Opening times: daily (except Tues), Apr 1-Oct 31, 11am-5.30pm
Admission: adult £3.60; child £1.80; NT members free

WHERE TO STAY

Constantine Bay
🏠 ✕ 🐴 🛏 £££ ✗

Treglos Hotel, *Constantine Bay, near Padstow PL28 8JH*
Tel: 0841 520727
Open mid Mar-end Oct
People return year after year to this very comfortable white-washed hotel which stands in its own grounds above the bay. The bedrooms and suites are wonderfully light and airy and tastefully decorated in peaches and greens. There is an attractive heated indoor pool and Jacuzzi, and the patio overlooking the bay is a popular place for tea or an early evening drink. Rooms are priced on a half-board basis and the restaurant offers good English and French cooking with an extensive hors d'oeuvre buffet followed by soup, roasts and fresh fish. Jacket and tie is required for dinner. Non-residents should make reservations. Last orders for dinner 9pm.

Padstow

🏠 🐴 ▭ ££ 🚶

Old Custom House Inn, *South Quay,*
Padstow PL28 8ED
Tel: 0841 532359
Closed Jan & Feb
There is a dearth of hotel accommodation in Padstow, and this former
grain store and custom house overlooking the harbour is a pleasant,
reasonably priced place to stay,
although in summer those who like
an early night may find the noise of
revellers drifts up from the quay.
Bedrooms are simply but tastefully
furnished, most with shower rooms,
and the restaurant has a good reputation for its fresh fish and seafood.
Last orders for dinner 9.30pm.

Port Gaverne

🏠 ✕ 🐴 ▭ £££ 🚶

Port Gaverne Hotel, *near Port Isaac*
PL29 3SQ
Tel: 0208 880244
Closed mid Jan-mid Feb
Situated in a sheltered pebble cove
around a headland from Port Isaac,
this 17th-century inn has 18 comfortable bedrooms. Downstairs there are
beamed bars and a separate
restaurant which serves locally reared
beef and lamb as well as fish and
seafood. A cheaper alternative is to
eat from the bar menu, available at
lunchtimes and in the evening. In
summer there is seating outside
beside a quiet road. Last orders:
lunch 2pm; dinner 10pm.

Port Isaac

🏠 ✕ 🐴 ▭ ££ 🚶

The Slipway Inn, *Port Isaac PL29 3RH*
Tel: 0208 880264
Open all year
This 16th-century inn beside the
harbour beach is a characterful place
with steep staircases and odd-shaped
rooms tucked under the eaves.
Bedrooms are on the small side but
prettily furnished, some with
attached bathrooms. There are car
parking spaces in front of the inn.
Downstairs there is a cosy, comfortable bar and a galleried restaurant,
open to non-residents. Bar snacks are
served at lunchtimes; the à la carte
dinner menu is strong on fresh fish
and seafood, especially lobster and
crab in season. Indian-inspired dishes
are the order of the day on Mondays.
Last orders: lunch 2.15pm; dinner
9.30pm.

St Newlyn East

♿ 🍴 £ 🚶

Degembris Farm, *St Newlyn East,*
Newquay TR8 5HY
Tel: 0872 510555
Open Easter-end Oct
Situated four miles inland from
Newquay this listed slate-hung farmhouse dates back to the 18th century.
Kathy Woodley offers a warm
friendly welcome and the bedrooms
are prettily decorated in floral prints,
all with colour TV. The rooms do not
have en suite facilities but across the
hall are two large modern bathrooms,
one with a good shower closet.
Lovely countryside walks from the
farm.

WHERE TO EAT

Padstow
✕ ▭ ££££ ✕

The Seafood Restaurant, *Riverside,
Padstow PL28 8BY*
Tel: 0841 532485
*Dinner only; closed Sun and mid-Dec -
early Feb*

This is considered to be the finest restaurant in Cornwall - not that competition is fierce - and locals come from miles around to celebrate special occasions in the light, airy dining room. Rick Stein's cooking is delicious, his creative sauces making good use of herbs and there are some excellent pasta starters. Fish and seafood inevitably dominate the menu. Very good wine list. Upstairs there are 10 comfortable bedrooms, some with balconies and harbour views. Last orders for dinner 9.30pm.

Pendoggett
▦ ⋈ ▭ ££ ✕

The Cornish Arms, *Pendoggett, near
Port Isaac*
Tel: 0208 880263
Open all year

This old inn stands on the B3314, a surprisingly busy road, so we do not recommend staying here. However, the bars are very pleasant with slate floors and sturdy wooden furnishings. Expect large portions of good wholesome fare from the bar menu: seafood crêpes, fresh local lemon sole and lobster as well as beef stew and traditional liver, onion and bacon. Reasonable wine list, and good range of beers on hand pump. Last orders: lunch 2pm; dinner 9.30pm.

St Kew
▦ ⋈ ⊠ £ ✕6

St Kew Inn, *St Kew (signposted from
the A39)*
Tel: 0208 84259
Open all year

This handsome brick inn stands at the heart of an idyllic village and in summer its garden across the road beside the river is a peaceful place to enjoy a simple dinner and a drink. Inside there is a cosy, rustic bar and a separate dining room where children are allowed. The bar menu is imaginative and has an Indian flavour with onion bhajis and curries alongside crab and vegetable oriental parcels, fish pie and local sirloin steaks. Good on vegetarian dishes too. Last orders: lunch 2pm; dinner 9.30pm (9pm Sundays).

NORTH-EAST CORNWALL

There is no relief from the elements along this wild, windswept north-east coast. The trees are stunted and bent by exposure to the almost constant wind and the only safe harbour is the tiny inlet of Boscastle. But there is beauty in such bleakness: the cliffs, rising to 600ft in places, are spectacular and the sunsets glorious. Inland is another landscape with a rugged beauty all its own - Bodmin Moor. This corner of Cornwall is a place for those who love the outdoors and there are some beautiful walks along the cliffs, over moorland and through hidden wooded valleys.

This is the land of Arthurian legend and during the summer Tintagel and Boscastle are inundated with coach daytrippers, so try to arrive early or late in the day to appreciate their charms. If you are driving into Cornwall along the A30, Jamaica Inn is a popular lunch stop, although the Eliot Arms nearer Launceston serves better food and is popular with locals as well as with visitors. If you have children you may decide to head for the sands at Bude, another top surfing resort, or the Tamar Otter Park.

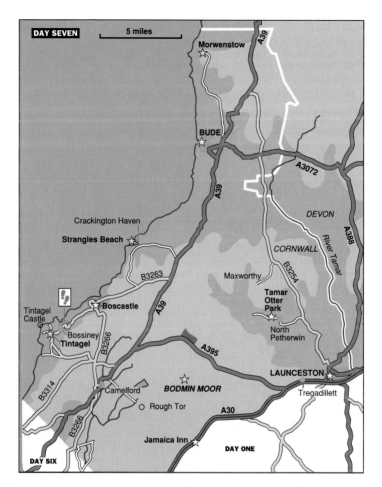

DAY SEVEN
5 miles

Morwenstow

A39

BUDE

A39

A3072

DEVON

A388

River Tamar

Crackington Haven

Strangles Beach

CORNWALL

B3254

B3263

Maxworthy

Tamar
Otter
Park

Boscastle

A39

Tintagel
Castle

B3266

North
Petherwin

Bossiney
Tintagel

A395

B3314

LAUNCESTON

Camelford

BODMIN MOOR

Tregadillett

○ Rough Tor

A30

B3266

Jamaica Inn

DAY ONE

DAY SIX

☆   BODMIN MOOR

These desolate granite uplands surmounted by brooding tors
have a strange, compelling beauty. Distance is foreshortened
under the huge skies and on a clear day you can see for miles.
While not as forbidding as Dartmoor, the treacherous marshes
of Bodmin Moor have claimed their share of victims over the
centuries. Even locals who know the moors well become disori-
entated when a heavy mist descends. The weather can change
suddenly here so if you are walking far from your car take

warm clothing, something to eat, and preferably a compass, even if there isn't a cloud in the sky.

Roughtor is the most easily accessible high point on the moor and a wonderful place for a picnic on a calm, sunny day. Turn off the A39 at Camelford, signposted Roughtor, and after two miles the road ends in a car park. The great boulder-encrusted tor rises straight ahead and the walk to the summit, across springy tussocks grazed by shy wild ponies, takes 30 minutes or so. The grey granite slabs, smoothed and weathered to resemble toadstool caps, appear to balance precariously on top of each other and provide a giant natural climbing frame for children. From this 1,000ft eyrie you feel on top of the county: a long stretch of the north coast unfolds beneath you, china clay pits scar the landscape to the east, and to the south is Brown Willy, the highest point in Cornwall.

View from the top of Roughtor, Bodmin Moor

If you prefer to see Bodmin Moor from the comfort of your car there is an evocative drive along its western flank via unfenced roads. Heading west on the A30 from Jamaica Inn, take the first right turn about three miles down the road, signposted St Breward. There are lovely views over the long yellow moorland grass towards tor-capped hills. At a T-junction in the hamlet of Bradford, turn left, then first right towards St Breward and cross a small river before carrying straight on to the village and its deeply rural pub, the Old Inn, which serves good bar lunches. From here you can wind further along the flank of the moor, eventually joining the road to Roughtor.

The **North Cornwall Museum and Gallery** in Camelford contains a diverse collection of all kinds of bygones and traditional workman's tools. Built up over 18 years by Sally Holden, who also runs the local **Tourist Information Centre** in the same building, it contains many items given to her father, the local doctor, by his patients. There are complete workshops which once belonged to tanners, clog- and shoemakers, printers and farriers, and displays on granite and slate mining in the area. Domestic artefacts include some of the first sewing machines, a reconstruction of a typical moorland cottage at the turn of the century, and examples of lace and embroidery. Upstairs there are changing exhibitions of work by local artists and potters.

North Cornwall Museum & Gallery, The Cleave, Camelford. Tel: 0840 212954
Opening times: daily, except Sun, Easter-Sept 30, 10am-5pm
Admission: adult £1; child 50p

☆ BOSCASTLE

A fjord-like cleft in the cliffs leads to the tiny harbour of Boscastle, the only place a ship could load in safety on 40 miles of coast. Today the village is almost entirely given over to tourism: the white-washed cob cottages are holiday homes, the old stables have become a youth hostel, and the inns and shops cater to an undiscerning clientele. There is even a shop specialising in pixies. Yet despite this rampant commercialism, Boscastle has charm. You can walk up around the headlands that guard the entrance to the harbour for magnificent views along the coast, and wander up from the harbourside car park to the village itself where narrow lanes are lined with mediaeval dwellings, all bulging walls and bowed slate roofs.

Beside the harbour is the **Museum of Witchcraft**, a long-established place which presents the case for witchcraft and black and white magic in a way which is both disturbing and amusing. Visitors are fascinated by the displays and the associated commentaries: waxworks of modern witches in action; all kinds of charms, talismen and potions, some picked up at local fairs in the Fifties; and broomsticks, clothes and dried toads said to have belonged to famous West Country witches.

Opening times: daily Easter-mid Oct 10am-5.30pm
Admission: adult £1; child 60p

Boscastle

> The beautiful **Valency valley** leads inland from Boscastle and is accessible only on foot. A pleasant two-mile walk through ancient coppiced woodlands alongside a river leads to the church at St Juliot, restored by Thomas Hardy, then a young architect, in the 1870s. He met his wife Emma Gifford here, and his novel *A Pair of Blue Eyes* is set in north Cornwall, although the place names have been changed.

☆ BUDE

Bude is a surfers' paradise and Crooklets Beach is known as Britain's Bondi. Lifesaving demonstrations are held on Tuesday evenings in summer and it is a popular venue for surfing championships. Families usually prefer to head for Summerleaze beach beside the entrance to Bude's canal which has an excellent seawater swimming pool washed by the tides. The town itself is a small place with the usual bucket-and-spade and surfing shops and terraces of turn-of-the-century guesthouses.

Bude's canal, built in 1826 to carry sand inland as far as Launceston, is an impressive feat of engineering with lock-gates leading directly into the sea. You can hire rowing boats to explore the mile or so that is still navigable and walk a further mile along the towpath which is rich in birdlife. There is excellent coarse fishing (the close season is April 1-June 1) and permits can be bought from the **Tourist Information Centre** in the Crescent Car Park; tel: 0288 354240. A former foundry beside the canal has been turned into the local historical and folk museum which has an interesting collection of old photographs showing Bude before the surfers arrived.

Bude Canal

Many churches in Cornwall suffered from Victorian 'restorers' but in the village of **Launcells** (off the A3072 east of Bude and Stratton) the church of St Swithins is a 15th-century gem. The graceful interior is suffused with light as the Perpendicular windows retain their original plain glass. It contains 60 carved bench-ends, the glory of the church, and in the chancel there are fine mediaeval clay tiles depicting griffins, lions, pelicans and flowers.

JAMAICA INN

Today Jamaica Inn is the most famous public house in Britain, an inn with its own bypass, souvenir pens and tea towels, and an acre of car parking. Catapulted to stardom by Daphne du Maurier's novel about the dastardly doings of Joss Merlyn and his gang of wreckers, it has never looked back. The idea came to du Maurier after she hired a horse from Jamaica Inn to ride on Bodmin Moor. Soon after setting out, rain and fog replaced sunshine, and she spent an agonising evening lost among the moor's disorientating bogs, quarries and boulders until her horse led her back to the inn. The success of her subsequent novel made du Maurier feel rather guilty about destroying the character of this 16th-century coaching inn, and in *Vanishing Cornwall* she writes: 'As a motorist I pass with some embarrassment, feeling myself to blame.... as an author I am flattered, but as a one-time wanderer dismayed.'

Humorous taxidermy from Potters Museum, Jamaica Inn

It is likely that Jamaica Inn, the only pub on the A30 between Launceston and Bodmin, would have changed anyway to cope with the modern influx of travel-weary holidaymakers seeking refreshment. While there is a large newish annexe to cater for the coach parties, the cosy bars in the original inn appear fairly authentic with flagstone floors, old settles and roaring log fires. The food isn't up to much but there's atmosphere here yet. The courtyard contains a Daphne du Maurier room with her desk, portraits of her family, a few belongings and foreign translations of her novels - one in Rumanian.

 Beside the inn, a new building contains **Potter's Museum of Curiosity**, recently moved here from its original home in Sussex. Assembled by taxidermist Walter Potter in the last decades of the 19th century, it contains a great profusion of exotic artefacts, stuffed birds and animals from around the world which would have enthralled Victorian visitors: from tribal masks and Whirling Dervish robes to South Seas earrings made from human bone and freaks such as a two-headed lamb and a four-legged chicken.

The Victorians were particularly fond of 'humorous taxidermy' and the museum contains a series of tableaux depicting athletic toads, duelling squirrels and guinea pigs playing cricket, as well as popular nursery rhymes and stories. Potter's favourite tableau, the Death and Burial of Cock Robin, contains 98 specimens of British birds. Modern-day curio lovers will find plenty to interest them, but the squeamish should pay a visit after lunch as some of the exhibits may take away your appetite.

Jamaica Inn open 11am-11pm, except Sun noon-3pm, 7-10.30pm; food served 11am-8.45pm
Museum of Curiosity open daily Easter-end Oct 9.30am-4pm (6pm in high summer)
Admission: adult £1.95; child £1.25

☆ LAUNCESTON

Cornwall's inland towns appear dull in comparison to the scenic delights of its coastal ports and villages. Launceston (pronounced 'Lanson' by locals) is an exception and a pleasant place to explore if the weather is inclement on the coast. It is an ancient town with origins predating the Norman Conquest and until 1838 it held the Right of Assize, and therefore the right to call itself the county capital. Even though it is no longer Cornwall's administrative centre, this is still the town to which succeeding Dukes of Cornwall come to receive their feudal dues. The Cornwall Heritage Project has published a useful booklet, *Launceston Town Trail Walkabout*, which will guide you around the pick of its sights and historic buildings. It is available from the **Tourist Information Centre** in Market Street; tel: 0566 772321.

Towering over the roof-tops is **Launceston Castle**, built in the early years of the Conquest to keep a grip on the hostile population. From the top of the keep there are commanding views over the town and a swathe of countryside beyond, but little of interest inside to justify the admission cost. You can appreciate its strategic location and ruins for free from the small park in which it stands. Facing away from the castle, turn right through north gate into Castle Street which is lined with some fine Georgian town houses.

One of these, Lawrence House, now contains the **Launceston Museum**. It is not an exceptional place but you could while away an hour here on a rainy day. The ladies who look after it, on a voluntary basis, are full of information on Launceston and keen to tell the stories behind their favourite pieces. As well as all the usual domestic bygones and personal belongings, it contains the feudal dues presented to Prince Charles which include a bundle of twigs, a goatskin and a bowl of pepper! Of little value to a modern prince, they remain on display here. Another exhibit of interest is a Victorian polyphant, a forerunner of the record player, which plays circular steel discs if you insert 10p.

The museum is open from Apr 1-mid Oct, Mon-Fri 10.30am-4.30pm.
Tel: 0566 773277
Admission free

Steam train enthusiasts should not miss a ride on the **Launceston Steam Railway** from Launceston Station. You can walk from the town centre or park in the old station yard. The locomotives were built in Victorian times and run on a two-foot gauge line. It's a jolly ride of a couple of miles through the wooded valley of the river Kensey in covered coaches. Adjoining the station is an exhibition hall and workshop where you can inspect those locomotives not in use at close quarters.

It also contains some steam-driven machinery, vintage cars and motorcycles. The Railway Buffet serves good freshly-made light meals and refreshments.

Launceston Steam Railway, Launceston Station. Tel: 0566 775665
Opening times: 10.30am-4.30pm Good Fri-Easter Mon, then Sun & Tues until
Whitsun, and during Oct; daily Whitsun-end Sept
Admission: adult £3.30; child £2.20 for unlimited rides

☆ MORWENSTOW

At the height of the summer, the hamlet of Morwenstow is a delightful tranquil refuge from the crowds. It comprises a few ancient farmsteads, a pub, church and vicarage set between two narrow coombs whose rivers end as cliff waterfalls. Inside the church there are some particularly fine Norman arches carved with bearded men, birds and dogs. The Victorian Gothic vicarage beside it was built by the eccentric vicar and poet, R S Hawker, who modelled its chimneys on church towers and his mother's gravestone. The present owners now take in guests (see Where to Stay).

Hawker, who once masqueraded as a seaweed-clad mermaid sitting on a rock and singing falsetto in the moonlight, has a special place in Cornish hearts. His ballad *The Song of the Western Men* has become the modern Cornish anthem. It celebrates Bishop Trelawny's refusal to sign James II's Declaration of Indulgence giving greater freedom of worship to dissenters. (Ironically Hawker converted to Roman Catholicism on his deathbed.) Two verses give the gist of its appeal to the independent-minded Cornish:

A good sword and a trusty hand
A merry heart and true
King James's men shall understand
What Cornish lads can do...

And when we come to London Wall
A pleasant sight to view
Come forth! come forth! ye cowards all:
Here's men as good as you...

Hawker is also credited with reviving the Harvest Festival service, now celebrated in churches around the world. The driftwood hut where he wrote his poetry is preserved by the National Trust and can be visited by walking through the gate beside the churchyard down to the sea and turning left along the coastal path. After viewing the simple hut, carry on along the path and turn inland again up the Tidna valley to reach Morwenstow's inn, a circular walk of one-and-a-half miles.

The **Bush Inn** lays claim to be one of the oldest in Britain and appears little altered since the built-in settles and massive fireplace were installed. The bar food is simple but freshly made and served at lunchtimes only (not Sunday). On fine days you can relax in the cobbled courtyard or on the grass beyond. Opposite the church, Rectory Farm serves refreshments and cream teas in summer.

☆ STRANGLES BEACH

The 650ft cliffs rising from Strangles Beach near Crackington Haven are the highest in Cornwall. Their extraordinary height is matched by their beauty and to admire their variegated colour and texture you can take a footpath down to the seashore from opposite Trevigue Farm (see Where to Stay). It is a strenuous but not overly steep walk as it follows the path of an ancient track used by donkeys hauling sand and slate from the beach. The cliffs, almost sheer in places, are composed of an easily fractured shale, its brown and grey strata bent and contorted in a myriad ways. Where landslips have created hollows, gorse and heather thrive. On the sand and pebble beach, where you can swim in calm conditions, lonely stacks and arches testify to the sea's victories over the land.

☆ TAMAR OTTER PARK

Otters are shy, secretive, nocturnal creatures and this small nature park provides a chance to see them at close quarters. Hunted for their pelts and killed by poisonous pesticides, otters are on the endangered list in England and Wales and this sanctuary, run by the British Otter Trust, is successfully breeding otters and reintroducing them to the wild. The breeding pens are set around dammed ponds and on sunny days visitors can see the otters snoozing on their banks. The wooden holts alongside are usually open to visitors and contain new-born offspring, curled up in the hay beside their mothers. The otters - both Asian short-clawed and British - are fed on a diet of fish at noon, 3.30pm and just after 5pm.

In the bushes nearby there is the incongruous sight of Australian red-necked wallabies which are also being bred. Wild ducks and geese visit the water fowl lakes and beautiful golden pheasants and peacocks strut around the pens. A gate leads through to the woods where the fallow deer and rabbits show no fear and, dotted among the trees, are aviaries for breeding five species of British owls, arranged in such a way that you can nearly always get a sight of these nocturnal creatures. A pleasant café provides refreshments, home-made cakes and pasties.

Tamar Otter Park and Wild Wood, signposted from North Petherwin near Launceston.
Tel: 0566 85646
Opening times: daily Apr 1-Oct 31, 10.30am-6pm
Admission: adult £3; children 4-16 £1.50

☆ ## TINTAGEL

Most people come to Tintagel because of its Arthurian connections. It must once have been a tranquil place of great beauty: a small hamlet on a castle-crowned headland with commanding views over a splendid coastal landscape. The Victorian romantic poets caused all this to change, firing the imaginations of the public who descended in their droves to stay in the distinctly unromantic boarding houses which now straggle over the headland towards King Arthur's Castle Hotel. The enormity and ugliness of this Victorian tourist hotel led to a local appeal against further development, and in 1897 the rest of the headland was purchased by the newly formed National Trust, its first coastal property in England.

There is no archaeological evidence to suggest that Tintagel was the birthplace of King Arthur or the seat of a Cornish king, and the fanciful account by 12th-century court chronicler Geoffrey of Monmouth can be seen as a piece of nationalist propaganda. It was designed to give the Anglo-Norman kings a hero to help unite the English and provide a rival to the very real 8th-century French king Charlemagne and the epic songs surrounding his wars which still inspired French soldiers in battle. The legends surrounding King Arthur and the Knights of the Round Table together with the grandeur of the scenery around Tintagel captured the romantic imagination of a host of Victorian poets and artists, from Turner and Tennyson to Arnold and Swinburne, who revived and expanded on mediaeval legend.

Old Post Office, Tintagel

Tintagel remains one of Cornwall's chief tourist honeypots, its narrow main street busy with coaches and cars all summer. Although the shops selling plastic Merlins and Excaliburs and the cheap 'n' cheerful tea-rooms may be off-putting, Tintagel has several sights to interest the more discerning visitor. A narrow lane lined with herringbone slate walls leads from the tourist ghetto up to **Tintagel Castle**. Here, away from the crowds and the village you can appreciate the great beauty of this place in both sunshine and showers when the mist comes down and the surf thunders against the cliffs far below. The ruined walls of the 12th-century castle appear as natural extensions of the rocks on which they stand so precariously. Very steep and, in wet weather, slippery stairs plunge down to cross a narrow isthmus to 'the island' and the rest of the castle ruins. The fabulous views along the north coast as far as Lundy Island and Hartland Point in Devon are worth the strenuous walk, and you can leave via a small cove from where, in summer, a Landrover ferries the weary back up to the village.

Tintagel Castle, Tintagel. Tel: 0840 770382
Opening times: daily 10am-6pm Easter-Sept 30; 10am-4pm in winter, closed Sun
Admission: adult £1.60; child 80p

Looking like a curious anomaly in Tintagel's main street, **The Old Post Office** is a rare survival of a 14th-century domestic dwelling. It has been owned by the National Trust since 1903 which probably saved it from developers. Beneath its deeply bowed slate roofs there is a hall open to the roof, a parlour and two bedrooms, furnished with oak pieces brought from farmhouses in the area. You get a real flavour of what a mediaeval gentleman's home must have been like, and the counter of the Victorian post office it once was can be still seen. At the rear there is a pretty flower garden.

Opening times: daily Apr 1-Oct 31, 11am-5.30pm
Admission: adult £1.90; child 95p; NT members free

Behind the plain façade of a substantial Victorian house on the main street are the intriguing **King Arthur's Great Halls**. They are the creation of Frederick Glasscock, a millionaire custard manufacturer, who came to Tintagel in the 1920s and was seduced by the Arthurian romances. Using local workmen he erected King Arthur's Hall and the Hall of Chivalry and founded the Fellowship of the Round Table to revive the ideals of mediaeval chivalry. It may all sound rather far-fetched, but if you want to brush up on the legend of King Arthur this is a good place to come. The 11-minute show, narrated by Robert Powell alias Merlin, gives the bones of the legend as spotlights focus in turn on paintings, done by William Hatherell in 1928, illustrating critical moments in Arthur's life.

From here doors open into the Hall of Chivalry, an unexpectedly large handsome place. Many different kinds of Cornish stone were used in its building and the quality of the craftsmanship is superb. Two thrones and, of course, a replica of the Round Table dominate the hall, but its glory is the magnificent stained glass. The 73 windows, all made by Veronica Whall, a pupil of William Morris, were designed to convey the symbolic and spiritual meaning of the story of King Arthur. The figures are beautifully drawn and, when the sun shines, the hall is suffused with a kaleidoscope of colour.

King Arthur's Great Halls. Tel: 0840 770526
Opening times: daily Easter-end Oct 10am-5pm (last show 4.30pm)
Admission: adult £2.20; child £1.60

Pubs with sea views are rare on the north coast but at **Trebarwith Strand**, a couple of miles south of Tintagel, you can enjoy a good pub lunch on a terrace overlooking this popular bathing beach. The Port William serves home-made soups and pasties, fresh herrings and seafood dishes as well as a daily vegetarian special. In summer it is open all day for drinks. Last orders for food: lunch 2.30pm (2pm Sunday); dinner 9.30pm.

The Hall of Chivalry, King Arthur's Great Halls, Tintagel

ROCKY VALLEY WALK

Leave the daytrippers in Tintagel behind and drive out of the village to Bossiney, half-a-mile away. Park in the small car park on the left where a sign says 'Dogs worrying or chasing sheep will be shot'. Go through the wooden gate in the wall and cross the field to reach the cliff-top footpath. Below in Bossiney Haven there are two lovely safe sandy beaches at low tide, reached down steep cliffside paths. Turn right to follow the footpath around the headland and down into Rocky Valley. It is a gorge in miniature: a slip of a stream tumbling over tiny waterfalls between tussocky banks and narrow ledges full of wild flowers. Further upstream look out for the Bronze Age labyrinth carvings near the ruined slate building. Beyond this is Trevillett Mill Trout Farm which serves light lunches and cream teas as well as selling its own smoked rainbow trout and trout pâté.

From here you can either turn right down the road back to the car or cross over and head up a steep lane to Halgabron. Just past the farm is a public footpath signposted St Nectan's Glen and Waterfall. Enter the deliciously cool woodlands which support a rich variety of ferns and flowers that flourish in damp conditions, and follow the riverside path up to the waterfall. It is hidden from the path and the owner of the bungalow charges visitors £1.50 for a view from the garden.

Retrace your steps to Halgabron and take the footpath signposted on the left of the lane which leads down over the fields and through the caravan park to Bossiney. The village contains some lovely old houses and is famous as being the most rotten of all the rotten boroughs, sending two MPs to Parliament until 1832, elected by just a handful of voters.

WHERE TO STAY

Boscastle

⌂ ✲ ▭ £ ☗12

St Christopher's Country House,
Boscastle PL35 0BD
Tel: 0840 250412
Open beg Mar-end Oct
Situated high above the harbour in
the old village, this Georgian house
stands in a quiet terrace away from
the main road. It is a comfortable,
homely place to stay and its increasing popularity makes it wise to book
ahead in summer. All the comfortable bedrooms, bar one, have
attached bathrooms. Good home
cooking is served in the dining room
and there's a sitting room for guests'
use.

Crackington Haven

⌂ ✉ £ £ ☗12

Trevigue Farm, *Crackington Haven,*
Bude EX23 0LQ
Tel: 0840 3418
Open Mar 1-Sept 30
Good hotels are hard to come by in
north-east Cornwall, but there are
some excellent farm guesthouses. A
few hundred yards from the spectacular Strangles Beach, reached down a
steep cliff path, this fortified farm set
around a cobbled courtyard dates
from the 16th century. Upstairs,
beneath ancient beams, there are four
lovely large bedrooms, handsomely
furnished with antiques; all have en
suite bathrooms. The cosy sitting
room with its old leather chairs has
an open fire and Janet Crocker's food
enjoys a good reputation: home-
made soups, venison in red wine,
steak and kidney pie and good old-
fashioned English puddings. Table
licence.

Maxworthy

⌂ ✉ £ ☗

Wheatley Farm, *Maxworthy,*
Launceston PL15 8LY
Tel: 0566 81232
Open Easter-end Sept
In a deeply rural setting near the
Tamar Otter Park, this substantial
Victorian farmhouse is one of a number built by the Duke of Bedford for
his estate workers. The bedrooms are
handsomely decorated with lovely
modern bathrooms; two have bunk
beds for children. Valerie Griffin's
farmhouse cooking is excellent, using
fresh produce wherever possible,
including traditionally reared beef
and lamb and rainbow trout. The
clotted cream and unpasteurised
green top milk come from their own
dairy. There's a snooker room for
adults, a laundry room, and a cellar
playroom for children who are welcome to watch the milking and 'help
out' on the farm under supervision.

Morwenstow

⌂ ✉ £ ☗

The Old Vicarage, *Morwenstow, near*
Bude EX23 9RS
Tel: 0288 83369
Closed Dec
You can now stay in the Victorian
vicarage built by the eccentric
Reverend Hawker as house guests of
Richard and Jill Wellby. A delightful
tranquil spot, the vicarage has distant
sea views and a short walk across the
fields brings you to the coastal path.
There are two tastefully furnished
doubles and a single, all with their
own bathrooms. Downstairs guests
have the use of a sitting room and the
library. Dinner is served at 8pm and
guests are encouraged to meet over a
complimentary drink beforehand.